RELIGION
IN RUSSIA

RELIGION IN RUSSIA

By

ROBERT PIERCE CASEY

Brown University

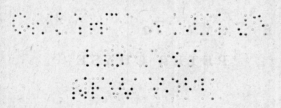

HARPER & BROTHERS

NEW YORK   *PUBLISHERS*   LONDON

To

PETER CHASE

CONTENTS

PREFACE

THIS BOOK CONTAINS THE LOWELL LEC-
tures, delivered at King's Chapel in Lent, 1945. The text of the
lectures as delivered has hardly been altered. An epilogue has
been added to include a brief survey of the rapidly moving
events in Russian Church history in the last year. Footnotes
have been reduced to a minimum and a bibliography has been
omitted as the sources have been mainly Russian. The specialist
will easily identify or discover them; the English reader will not
be helped by English transcriptions of the Russian titles of books
he cannot use. Contemporary works on Russia have, for the
most part, been written to prove something. Their authors are
advocates or enemies of Communism, travelers who have
known Russia in the old days and have returned to experience
disillusionment or a happy surprise, or newcomers desirous to
learn or to confirm long-standing prejudices. My interest has
been simply that of a historian who, with a certain skepticism
of the possibility of judging the contemporary scene fairly, has
read widely in Russian and other sources, talked with people
who have been in Russia recently and long ago, and has attempted to retell what he has read and heard with the same kind
of imagination and common sense he would have applied to
any other historical problem.

No book, however, is written without private enthusiasms.
My first has been as a teacher who believes it vitally important
for young Americans to know as much as possible the life of a
working partner in the reconstruction of a world which will

certainly not be wholly new nor wholly brave but must be built co-operatively, if it is to be a cosmos at all. My second enthusiasm is that of a priest of a communion deeply friendly to Russian Orthodoxy and greatly desirous to see and, if may be, help in its rebuilding. It is a happy circumstance that in religion an aim is not judged by the means or the measure of its fulfillment. In Russia, to my mind, the aim of the Church is clear and accurate. Whether and how it will be reached is neither the business of the historian to prophesy nor of the priest to judge.

My thanks are due to the Trustees of the Lowell Institute for their invitation, and to the following for their help in investigation or in the criticism and preparation of my manuscript: Dean and Mrs. Willard L. Sperry, Professor Arthur D. Nock, Professor Michael Karpovich, all of Harvard University; my colleagues Professors Benjamin Brown and Joachim Wach of Brown University; Mr. Paul Anderson and Mr. Alexander Kasem-Beg of the New York City Y.M.C.A.; Archimandrite Cyril (Johnson), Dr. William V. Silverberg and Mr. Howard L. Cowan. The *Review of Religion* of Columbia University has kindly allowed me to reproduce material from two review articles of mine in the issues of May, 1944, and March, 1945. The American representative of Preslit Literary Agency, New York City has generously approved the use of my translations from books published recently in the Soviet Union and International Publishers of my quotations from their translation of F. Engels' *Ludwig Feuerbach*.

RELIGION
IN RUSSIA

Chapter I

THE IMPERIAL CHURCH

IN 1843 MARX WROTE IN HIS REVIEW OF HEGEL'S *Philosophy of Law,* "For Germany the criticism of religion is essentially ended and the criticism of religion is the basis of all criticism." The thesis that Christianity was done for and that religious tradition was a dying factor in human society was not the invention of Marx. It represented the convictions of the more radical French Encyclopedists and received frequent expression time and again from the pen of Voltaire; it found many defenders among the English rationalists and was taken over as a dogma by the German materialists. In the eighteenth century an ebullient atheism was a philosophic mode; in the nineteenth century it became a widely held philosophic creed.

In spite of massive adherence to this view among educated men and an effective popularization of materialist views, Christianity did not die nor did religion lose its hold on society. In France a wide breach was effected between traditional religion and secular philosophy, though currents of more liberal religious thought were not lacking. In England the nineteenth century was a period of vigorous religious activity. Both the Oxford Movement and the Evangelical Revival were in part defensive and reactionary, but neither left English religion where it found it and both contributed to its vitality. The Established Church gained, rather than lost, influence even among educated men. In Germany, more than in England, there was a flowering of religious philosophy in the universities and a renaissance of church life, especially in the north. In Italy in the second half of the nineteenth century a secular state was established and its growth was accompanied by a *risorgimento* of culture. The prevailing philosophy was idealist and religious values were reworked and freshly expressed by men like Croce and Gentile. The Modernist crisis in the Roman Church evoked a new religious temper in the Church historian Buonaiuti, the novelist Fogazzaro, and a host of lesser men. In spite of continued warnings and the militancy of opposing tendencies, the early demise of Christianity did not occur and in the early twentieth century the arguments against Christianity, current for a century and a half, were uttered with a certain querulousness, as the baked meats prepared for the obsequies of this troublesome historical phenomenon threatened to grow stale and unpalatable.

The great war 1914–18 was a rude shock to religious sensibilities. Violent death, widespread pain and loss, following upon a period when optimism on social questions had been general and peace among nations an accepted convention, brought equally widespread questioning and disillusionment. The problem of theodicy suddenly became acute, personal immortality a burning issue, and the responsibility of the Church for a moral order which had proved so fragile and unreliable was bitterly debated. The theory of a limited God, whose heart was in the right place but whose effectiveness in the struggle against evil was a gamble, was taken over from the Pragmatists and Personal Idealists and made into a popular faith by H. G. Wells. Psychical research tried to convince where orthodoxy failed to reassure. The roots of social evil were sought not in man but in flaws in the social system. Men reached out to a brave new world, but their gestures were clutching and hysterical. Utopias were not carefully planned and left in mid-air, as in the eighteenth and nineteenth centuries, but were hastily executed, scrappily and on a small scale. Unconsidered experimentation was the order of the day. The lost generation of the twenties went down on a thousand ill-chosen moral battlefields, proving in their costly failures and small successes only what had always been known to be true about the elements of individual and social life.

In Russia the attack on religion came late and was due less to restless minds and thwarted emotions, than to social discontent on practical matters and a rough sense that old wrongs must be righted without delay. The assault on religion was frontal and was attractive to the man in the ranks, not through any shift in conviction, but because of long-standing resentment at the connivance of the Church as an institution with the oppressive tsarist state. The revolutionary leaders were materialists with a highly dogmatic cast of mind and they were able to impose their thoughts on others. The role of thought was, however, secondary and fused with the surge of revolutionary action. The fusion was important, for Lenin's materialism served not only as a justification of the revolt but as a blueprint for the new social order.

The attack on the Orthodox Church in Russia by the Bolsheviks was grounded on the assumption that the Church was the tool of the tsarist regime. The ferment which erupted in revolution was a protest against the social action of the imperial government; because the Church was a powerful factor in that social action and one of its most effective agents of propaganda and morale, it was a natural object of bitter criticism and violent attack. In order to understand the history of religion in Russia since the Revolution, it is necessary to examine the justice of the Bolshevik theory of the imperial Church and to survey briefly the historical development lying behind it.

The relations between Church and State in Russia had a somewhat different history than in the West. Many of the basic problems of theory and administration were the same, but history cast these relations in a different mold and the time schedule of Russian history lagged behind that of Western Europe by nearly two hundred years.

Christianity in Russia was an import from Constantinople, but for many centuries its importer kept a lien on his goods. The supreme ecclesiastical authority remained the patriarch of Constantinople, at least in theory, until 1589. The administrative structure of the Russian Church was determined by the Greek nomocanon and by the precedents of Byzantine canon law, and its administrative policies and decisions often emanated from the East.

In the matter of investitures the appointment of the metropolitan of Kiev and All-Russia was from the beginning in the hands of the patriarch of Constantinople. After the conversion of Russia was assured and the hierarchy established, he was usually more interested in selecting Greeks whom he could trust than in finding men able to speak Russian and conversant with Slavic affairs. The ecclesiastical administration was, however, so free of the secular government and the texture of Church life so closely woven that the system of ultimate dependence on the patriarch worked better than any alternative. The two exceptions occurring before the middle of the thirteenth century: the election of Hilarion (1051) under Yaroslav, and of Clement (1147) under Isaslav, served only to confirm the wisdom of the rule. Under the Mongol yoke, order was brought out of the chaos of the invasion by the firmness and intelligence of the metropolitans. The Tatars supported the spiritual power of Constantinople over the Church and granted the appropriate civil rights to the appointees from Constantinople on their arrival in Russia.

Bishops were elected theoretically in conformity with the will of the people, but were actually nominated by the local princes who served as their representatives. The local princes were jealous of their rights in this matter, but nominations must be confirmed by the metropolitan and occasionally by the patriarch, a precaution which proved its usefulness under the confused conditions of Mongol domination. Bishops could be deprived of their sees for maladministration on the recommendation of the local princes. At all times the dioceses, or eparchies as they were called, were subject to regular visitation and inspection by the metropolitan or his representatives, who examined the accounts, received reports on the spiritual and temporal conditions of the diocese, heard complaints, and presided over the ecclesiastical courts in session during their stay. In general the power of the bishops corresponded with that prescribed by Greek canon law. With the approval of the secular authorities, bishops had legal jurisdiction over the clergy and other Church officials, including the people employed on Church lands as well as the personnel of the monasteries. Charges of heresy against the laity, breaches of ecclesiastical discipline, and theft of Church property, cases involving the legality of marriages, the rights of parents over children and the laws of inheritance, and disputes over correct weights and measures in trade—all these were heard in the episcopal courts with rights of appeal in certain cases to the metropolitan. Disputes between bishops were decided by the metropolitan, or in case of need by the patriarch. The metropolitans consulted in matters of grave dispute with other bishops called in council for the purpose.

The lower clergy included seculars or White (robed) and monastics or Black (robed). The former were married before their ordination and lived with their families in the parishes to which they were elected or assigned. As elsewhere, a considerable variety prevailed among the monastic institutions both in administration and in the types of religious rule. The most popular was the famous Studite rule which was imported from Constantinople and adapted to Russian needs in the eleventh century.

The clergy, both lower and higher, secular and monastic,

were supported by regular taxes on the produce of the land, grants by the princes and nobles, and gifts and foundations of various sorts. As a rule the parish clergy were miserably underpaid and supported their large families in penury. The monasteries were the frequent recipients of large gifts and enjoyed a constant income from the contributions of pilgrims and pious visitors.

After the release from Tatar domination Russian politics took a new turn toward centralization and a more sweeping autocracy. The lead was taken by the princes of Moscow and followed by the metropolitans who had transferred their see, after the destruction of Kiev (1240) by the Tatars, first to Vladimir and then (1325) to Moscow. Curiously enough the government and the Church were drawn more closely together by the rise of the Muscovite state. Political centralization operated in favor of a more effective co-operation between the spiritual and temporal heads instead of increasing tension between the two, as was generally the case in the West. Under the Tatar yoke the Church flourished and vastly increased in wealth and influence, for it had been left largely to its own devices and singularly free in the administration of its own possessions and affairs. At the end of this period, so unfavorable to Russian social and political life as a whole, the Church emerged as the richest and most powerful organization in Russia, upon the co-operation of which the rebuilders of the Russian state had heavily to count.

The alliance between the metropolitans and the Great Princes of Moscow was a working agreement based on a community of interests. The Princes wanted the support of the Church in their move to centralize political power in Moscow and in combating the rival claims of other princes and the boyars or landed nobility. The metropolitans and bishops had always acted as mediators in such disputes but had preserved political neutrality. This neutrality was now abandoned, and not only moral suasion, but the powerful instruments of interdiction and excommunication were freely employed against the enemies of the Muscovite tsars. The Church, for its part, wanted to consolidate the gains it had made under the Tatar yoke and to protect its large estates against the predatory dispositions of the secular landowners and local nobility. This security could be effectively guaranteed only by Moscow.

Obviously such an arrangement could not work in the long run without friction, and the stage was set for a new era of rivalry between the metropolitans and the tsars. Dmitri Donskoi attempted to impose his candidate for the metropolitanate first upon the dying Metropolitan Alexei and then upon the clergy, but he met with resolute opposition and an appeal to the authority of the patriarch of Constantinople. The Prince's nominee died before the case was decided, but both sides had tried out the ground of controversy and tested their weapons of offense and defense.

The position of the Great Princes was indirectly strengthened by the disagreements between the Russian and the Greek Churches over the concessions made by the latter to Rome at the Council of Florence (1439), and even more by the patriarch's loss of prestige on the fall of Constantinople (1453). The Russian theory was that the occupation by the Turks was a punishment of the Greeks for their behavior at Florence and that in any case, since Constantinople was in the hands of the Turks, the patriarch was no longer to rule the Church. Moscow was the third Rome which had succeeded to the rights and dignities of the older ecclesiastical capitals and was destined to maintain its position until the end of the world. The rights of the patriarch in the appointment of the Russian metropolitan were therefore ignored and the candidate chosen by a *sobor* of Russian bishops.

The advantages of this situation from the imperial point of view were seen by Ivan III. The formulae of investiture were altered to state or imply the tsar's right to confer that office upon its recipient, e.g., "*H* has been elected and appointed by divine grace and at the desire of the sovereign, the Great Prince Ivan Vasilievich of All-Russia and on the recommendation of the holy fathers and archbishops. . . ." Metropolitan Zosimus was elevated to his high office by imperial decree without the formality of a council, but the choice proved an unhappy one and the tsar was obliged to force the resignation of his favorite after a short term of office. Encouraged by a grant of half the monastic and episcopal lands of the unhappy diocese of Novgorod by its bishop Theophil, Ivan III conceived the idea of taking all Church property under his direction and of thus relieving the clergy of the burden of its administration. The suggestion was made coyly to a council from which the tsar tactfully absented himself and was politely but firmly turned down. The plan, however, had been formulated and seriously intended and was not forgotten by Ivan III's successors. From this time on the thought of the Church's temporalities in the minds of the tsars was accompanied by a certain itching of the palm.

The reign of Ivan IV witnessed a national reform of the civil rights of the Church. At the Council of One Hundred Chapters and at a second council in 1551 the tsar succeeded in winning at least the formal consent of the Church for a series of radical changes in the legal status of the Church. Its rights to acquire landed property were curtailed and imperial grants of recent years rescinded. The jurisdiction of the secular and ecclesiastical courts was redefined and the powers of the latter enlarged. The regulation of Church business and the exercise of its secular rights and privileges were brought more closely under the control of the government. In a word, the first big step was taken to nationalize the Church and to integrate its administration with the government of the state.

This promising attempt to absorb the Church into the state

and reduce its administration to what in terms of its English counterpart has been called "a consecrated branch of the civil service" received a rude, if brief, check in the reign of Ivan IV's son, Theodore. The new tsar was a pious weakling who left the affairs of state largely in the hands of his father-in-law, Boris Godunov. Perhaps in despair at the tsar's ineffectiveness, Boris, as the power behind the throne, gave his support to a project of the tsar's to transform the Russian metropolitanate into an independent patriarchate. The Patriarch of Constantinople, Jeremiah, was not in a position to oppose this move nor was he disposed to do so, as he was in exile, in danger of his life and glad to find refuge under the protection of a powerful and friendly Christian prince. He consented willingly to the plan of Theodore and Boris Godunov and graciously presided over the enthronement of Job as the first patriarch of Moscow on his visit to that city in 1589.

Upon the death of Theodore political chaos ensued and the patriarch intervened as the highest authority in State and Church. He utilized his influence in this interregnum to bring Boris Godunov to the throne. Boris, in spite of his willingness to see the metropolitan elevated to a patriarchate, showed no inclination to welcome his appointee as a co-partner, much less as a rival, to his own autocratic power. It is possible that he had sensed the dangers of a too ecclesiastically controlled state during the patriarchal interregnum. It is, however, not impossible that he saw from the start that independence from the control of Constantinople carried with it the loss of extra-Russian interference in the Russian Church and so gambled on the power of the state to keep the new Russian patriarchate under its control. In the Patriarch Job he found a staunch supporter and a willing tool. In a communication addressed to the patriarch at the close of the Crimean campaign, the tsar greeted him pointedly as "supreme in *spiritual* matters." In his reply the patriarch described the tsar as "the true defender and administrator of the Christian faith." With this gesture the door was flung wide open for the occupation of the Church by the state under Peter the Great.

During the Period of Disturbances the patriarchate lost none of its rights and provided a much needed stabilizing force. The first Romanov, the Tsar Michael, elevated his own father to the patriarchate and entrusted him with broadest political powers. Michael's confidence was not misplaced. Although the Patriarch Philaret was no believer in hiding his light under a bushel and went even to the extent of associating his own name with that of his son on imperial decrees, his main interest lay in strengthening the tsar's position against the restless opposition of the boyars. He did not neglect the aggrandizement of his own office and the patriarchate regained much of the legal jurisdiction, especially in Church lands, which it had lost by the reforms of Ivan the Terrible. These gains were, however, short-lived and largely disappeared in the revised Code (*Ulozhenie*) issued by the Tsar Alexei Michailovich (1649).

In the early years of their association the role of Nikon at the court of Alexei Mikhailovich was not unlike that of Philaret and his son Michael Romanov. Nikon's interests were, however, quite different from those of his predecessor. He was first and last a churchman and was determined to use his ascendancy over the tsar to secure for the Church absolute sovereignty in its own sphere, including its temporalities and for the patriarch absolute sovereignty over the Church. He wished to sever the Church, its dependents and its lands completely from the jurisdiction of the state and to restore all the privileges it had lost in the successive reforms since Ivan III. It seems likely that he would have succeeded, had not the boyars learned their lesson from the reign of Michael Romanov and seen that a close alliance between the tsar and the patriarch could only work to their disadvantage, and that the removal of the Church from imperial control prevented the realization of their own ambitions and permitted the latter to increase and multiply its already great power and possessions. In achieving their aim to alienate the tsar from Nikon and finally to bring about his deposition, they prevented any important change in the legal position of the Church and kept it subordinate to the state in temporal matters.

The shock given to Erastian sensibilities by the exaggerated claims of Nikon for the patriarchate did not end with his personal defeat. It stood as a warning to future statesmen and was one of the factors in the decision of Peter the Great to include among his reforms a thoroughgoing subordination of the Church to the State. In 1700 the Patriarch Adrian died and was replaced by a locum tenens, Stefan Yavorskii, whose great but frustrated talents proved so useful a factor in Peter's maneuvers. This situation was prolonged until the tsar announced that there would be no patriarch. He had decided to abolish the office and to substitute for it a new representative assembly.

Since the form given to the relations between Church and State by Peter remained essentially untouched until 1917, we must give some consideration to the success and operation of his ecclesiastical program.

Neither by temperament nor by early training was Peter the Great disposed to a personal attachment to religion. As a child he was brought up in the practice of Orthodoxy, the forms of which he observed throughout his life. Before adolescence, however, he was isloated from the ecclesiastical influences of the court by his mother's move to the village of Preobrazhensk, where Peter surrounded himself with a band of young muckers over whom both his position and personality gained an easy ascendancy. His time was spent in their company organizing the military games which were the forerunners of his later reforms of Russia's army and navy and in cultivating the vices which his violent nature and fertile imagination suggested. In this he was encouraged by his tutor, the Swiss Lefort, a libertine of exotic tastes and great resourcefulness who used his influence on the young prince to corrupt his morals and infect his mind with his own cynical adaptations of Western European rationalism. Out of the orgies practiced under Lefort's benevolent eye in the addition made to his house at Peter's expense, arose the revolting parades of religious observances and ecclesiastical persons with which the tsar continued to enliven his entertainments throughout his life. Because he was interested in everything, he was interested in theology and enjoyed theological discussions, especially, with intelligent foreigners on his trips abroad. When in England in 1698 he recorded in his diary a conversation on "the Greek faith" with a group of Anglican bishops at Lambeth. Bishop Burnet, the historian, was one of his closest English friends. There was, however, small trace of personal piety in the tsar. Court gossip recalled that his dying words were not inappropriately, "Lord, help thou my unbelief."

Peter had a profound appreciation of the importance of religion as a social force, one which he proposed to keep alive among his people and direct to his own ends. His extensive trips to Western Europe opened his eyes to the possibility of reform in this as well as in other areas of national life, and he was not slow to see the advantages of the control over religion exercised in Protestant countries like England and Germany with their state churches and politically complacent ecclesiastics. It is impossible to say whether he learned more from England or Germany in this regard. German influence was strong among his theological advisers, notably Prokopovich, his friend and confidant in religious matters. Peter, however, had kept his eyes open in England and the constitution of the church envisaged in the *Duchovnyi Reglament* in some points resembles the English Establishment more than Lutheranism.

For a time Peter considered an alliance with the Pope. He received and gave attentive consideration to a suggestion for reunion by the theological faculty of the Sorbonne, but rejected it. He even sent a personal ambassador to Rome to survey the scene there, but reports on the operation of the papal system were too much for him. The Pope was a patriarch who would be unamenable to the tsar and could not be deposed.

There can be no doubt that Peter's religious policy was directed to the same end as his civil policies: the centralization of power in the tsar and the subjection of all branches of government and national life to his sovereign will. In 1718 Peter introduced a sweeping constitutional reform, abolishing a number of the old ministries and replacing them with "colleges" for foreign affairs, war, the admiralty, commerce, etc., the functions of which were defined in a statement of general instructions. In 1721 Peter issued the Ecclesiastical Instructions by which a new "college" was set up for the regulation of ecclesiastical affairs. In Part III, Section 2 of this remarkable document it is said, "With regard to the procedure of the Ecclesiastical College, there is nothing special to be said, since His Imperial Majesty has decreed that this college should proceed in the management of its affairs in conformity with the General Instructions." In defining the powers of the High Procurator, a new ecclesiastical official, the text of the General Instructions prescribing the duties of the High Procurator of the Senate was exactly reproduced with merely a change of the title in question. Apparently as an afterthought and obviously as a sop to wounded clerical sentiment the Ecclesiastical College was dignified by the more seemly title, "The Most Holy Synod," but the earlier description betrays the tsar's conception of its functions, a conception which dominated later imperial legislation.

The Ecclesiastical Instructions are an amazing agglomerate. Their author was the tsar's favorite ecclesiastic, Theophan Prokopovich, whose own ideas, especially on theology and religious education, are reflected in the text, but Peter kept an eye on the work and subjected it at some points to revision in his own inimitable manner. He and Theophan were at one in deploring the prevalence of gross superstition in the Russian Church and in their sympathy with the liberal ideas of the *Aufklärung*. The bitter allusions to the ignorance and incompetence of the clergy are phrased with Peter's brutal directness. The main concern of the tsar was, however, without doubt the clear statement of the relations of Church and State. He it was who proposed to abolish the patriarchate and to substitute for it a governing body appointed by himself and subject at all points and in all decisions spiritual and temporal to his sovereign will.

The decree promulgating the Ecclesiastical Instructions fixed the original personnel of the new college at eleven: a president, two vice-presidents, four councilors and four assessors. In the oath administered to its members are the unambiguous clauses, "[I swear] to bend all my energies to the furtherance of everything that conduces to the loyal service and advantage of His Imperial Majesty" and "I declare under oath that the supreme judge of this Ecclesiastical College is the monarch of All-Russia himself, our most gracious sovereign." In defining the competence of the new body the following points are mentioned: It is the primary business of the Synod to see that all the tsar's subjects remain in that state of life to which they are called and faithfully to fulfill its responsibilities. The Synod is to receive and pass on all suggestions for ecclesiastical reform. It is to exercise a rigorous censorship on all theological publications which may not be printed without its imprimatur. Claims of special revelations and experiences of miracles must be submitted to the Synod for judgment. Charges of heresy and schism and difficult cases of conscience, e.g., lapses into paganism under duress by prisoners of war are to be adjusted by the Synod. The character of candidates to the episcopacy must be investigated by the Synod and appeals from episcopal decisions may be made to it in cases of dubious marriages, divorce, and wrongs done by a bishop to his clergy, to the monasteries in his diocese or to another bishop. In this area the Synod takes over the jurisdiction formerly exercised by the patriarch. The Synod will oversee the administration of all Church property. In cases of wrong suffered by ecclesiastics at the hands of landlords the case will be tried by the civil authorities, but a report should be made to the Synod which will then lend its assistance to the grieved party. In testamentory disputes involving persons of rank, the case will be settled jointly by the Synod and the ministry of justice. The Synod is to issue instructions on the soliciting of alms and pious gifts to individuals. It is responsible for the abolition of simony and for proper provision for the parish clergy so that they will not traffic in fees for baptisms, marriages, and burials, though they may accept gifts.

In describing the episcopal office Peter gives acid expression to his jealousy of the outward respect paid to the higher clergy. Ironically, in view of the use of the anathema and interdict so helpful to the Muscovite Great Princes in earlier days, he wished this privilege rigorously controlled and its form and scope prescribed. The anathema might only be imposed with the written consent of the Synod and enforced by civil authority or appeal to the tsar. The interdict rested in the hands of the bishop whose conduct in such matters was, however, subject to correction by the Synod.

An ugly aspect of ecclesiastical as well as civil administration in Russia is reflected in the instruction on episcopal visitations, on the systematic use of official and unofficial espionage. Unfortunately this procedure is given every encouragement by the Ecclesiastical Instructions. Before opening the session of the episcopal court the bishop is to make full use not only of the reports of the diocesan inspectors, but of such private and confidential information as he can obtain openly or with guile, and the same methods are to be employed in investigating conditions in the monasteries. Reports on the state of the dioceses are to be made by each bishop to the Synod, even if there are no irregularities to be discussed. In quarrels between bishops or in cases of grievance against the bishop by the monastic clergy, appeal may be addressed to the Synod.

The portions of the Instructions which describe the new religious policy in general terms give a clear picture of the kind of social action envisaged by the tsars as appropriate to the Church. An enlightened, not an ignorant and superstitious, religious sentiment is to be fostered and the responsibility for encouraging and refining it is placed on the clergy. The reform must be implemented by improvements in clerical education, a tightening of standards for admission to Holy Orders, and by broader education for the laity. New schools must be founded and maintained at ecclesiastical expense, properly qualified teachers trained and employed, and brief popular manuals of instructions on the essentials of faith and morals, such as were in use among Protestants, should be composed and used at the Divine Liturgy and in the schools.

The money for these schools was to be levied by the bishop from the monasteries and when necessary from his own diocesan funds. Ostensibly to insure this, the bishop was required to present financial reports on his revenues and those of the monasteries to the Synod. When funds were inadequate, a more rigid economy was enjoined upon the bishops and monasteries. Indirectly this permitted a detailed supervision of diocesan and monastic properties and income.

It is impossible to enter here into the details of Prokopovich's scheme for an "academy" or university and for a preparatory school leading up to it, one of the principal functions of which was to provide better education for the clergy. Some of these ideas came into modified effect later on. More important are the requirements for the laity and civil authorities and their relation to the Synod. All the faithful are to be instructed in Christian doctrine and any interference with this is to be punished by the Synod. Communion is obligatory once a year, and those who absent themselves are to be considered in schism and reported by the bishop through the civil authorities to the Synod who will keep a register of such persons in each diocese. Landowners who secretly harbor schismatics are to be similarly delated. Schismatics may not hold ecclesiastical or civil office for fear of treasonous activity; it is therefore illegal to conceal unorthodox attachments and cases of this kind must be reported to the Synod. Private chapels even on great estates are forbidden. In electing a parish priest, the landlord, or, if he is not in residence, his dependents must guarantee his character and report on his salary. The incumbent must attach to this report a statement that he is content with his remuneration and will not leave. Landlords are forbidden the use of itinerant priests for confessors, must confess to the parish priest and must bring their children to him for baptism. The landlords must also respect the episcopal jurisdiction of the place in which they live and not appeal to another bishop. The Synod is the final authority in doubtful cases involving the prohibited degrees in marriage. All marriages must be blessed by the priest having local jurisdiction.

A word should be said about an unprecedented figure introduced on the ecclesiastical scene by Peter's reform: the High Procurator. Just as the Ecclesiastical College or Holy Synod was a replica of the other administrative colleges, so the High Procurator was a replica of the Procurator of the Senate. His function was to insure that business was conducted regularly, efficiently and according to law, and especially that the interests of the tsar were represented and carefully safeguarded. He is to keep his own minutes of proceedings and to see that decisions are carried out or their failure reported to the Synod or the tsar. He is to receive the reports of the diocesan inspectors on conditions in the different dioceses, present these to the Synod, and be sure that they are acted upon. The Procurator is subject to the tsar alone—except when he is absent, when the Synod has limited powers over him—and is described as the tsar's "eye" and as his legal representative in state affairs.

Theological and canonical considerations apart, the chief defect in Peter's new Church constitution was that he saw it through the rose-colored spectacles of his whole program of reform. The Church was bound hand and foot, signed, sealed, and delivered to the state, or rather to the autocratic will of the tsar. In this respect it did not differ from other branches of government, but whereas the latter were only affected relatively by the degree of control assumed by the tsar over the various departments of material life, the Church lost something of its essence. Its spiritual autonomy was gone and it could neither define truth nor prescribe conduct without interference. The tsar was *de jure* and *de facto* supreme arbiter in all decisions affecting faith and morals. Peter himself was so full of his plans for a new and better Russia that he did not see that the imperial control over the Church must work well or badly, depending on whether the tsar was a competent ruler and exercised an intelligent and responsible care of the Church or not. Churchmen like Yavorskii, first president of the Holy Synod, saw this very clearly and the soundness of their insight was confirmed by every phase of Church history from the death of Peter to the revolution of 1917.

The influence of the High Procurator also depended on the character of the man and that of the tsar he served. This office was charged with dynamite which exploded on more than one occasion. The combination of a weak tsar and strong Procurator could and did produce situations in which the Church was completely dominated by a lay pope devoid even of the sanctity traditionally associated with the imperial office. At best the High Procurator was a high-ranking imperial spy having under him a corps of agents composed of inspectors and employees of the Holy Synod, all of whom were under his charge.

At worst he became a flagrant usurper of the Church's natural rights, whose position could be justified only on the grounds of cynical statecraft.

The constitution of the Church and its relations to the state remained essentially unchanged from the death of Peter until 1917. The imperial government was not backward in exploiting its new power over the Church, especially in matters affecting politics and finance. It displayed no eagerness, however, in following up the educational program of the Ecclesiastical Instructions in the spirit of its authors or of fostering an enlightened religious sentiment. On the contrary, superstition and ignorance were tolerated and even encouraged, for the blind can be more easily led.

Regardless of personal interest or indifference in matters of religion, the successors of Peter the Great jealously guarded their supremacy over the Church and the subordination of its functions and functionaries to the secular bureaucracy. Under the pious Elizabeth Petrovna the hierarchy enjoyed the favor and patronage of the tsarina and the Holy Synod had both prestige and power, always under the watchful eye of the High Procurator. Catherine II, like Peter I, was an outsider to religion. Born a German and a Lutheran, her conversion to Orthodoxy was purely an affair of state. Dominated even more than Peter the Great by the ideas of the *Aufklärung,* her religious liberalism had no more relaxing effect upon the administration of the Church, than her early flirtations with political liberalism had upon her management of the state. She referred to her archbishops as "government officials" and her own "most loyal subjects," and counted heavily upon her High Procurators to see that the Synod remained nothing but the instrument of her decrees and the mouthpiece of her decisions.

In only one respect did she exercise any real religious toleration, viz., in her relations with dissenters and Roman Catholics. The minorities affected were, however, too small to have political importance. In the case of Roman Catholics, toleration wisely solved a difficult problem in the territories secured from dismembered Poland. Her friendliness toward Russian dissent may be explained in part as a reflex from her early Protestant upbringing, in part as a theatrical gesture designed to convince the connections she affected among West European intellectuals like Voltaire and Diderot of her enlightenment, in part as a warning to her Orthodox subjects that the wind of imperial favor blew where it listed.

A mortal stroke was dealt the independent economic power of the Church by the cool appropriation of the great bulk of the richest ecclesiastical lands by imperical decree. Curtis observes:

Vast areas with their serf populations were taken over by the state and in all 9,991,761 "souls" (males) and approximately the same number of females, or 13.8 per cent of all the peasants of Great Russia and Siberia. Thus in spite of the small lands left to the individual monasteries and the larger amount of comparatively worthless land in the north retained by the church, it ceased to be a great landholding institution. This secularization which was primarily intended to place great resources at the disposal of the state, had also the indirect effect of making the church even more dependent upon the state than before. The lands left in the possession of the churches and monasteries were so unproductive that the monasteries and the bishops had largely to rely on the small incomes paid them from the treasury in compensation for their lost land.[1]

The attitude of the Great Catherine toward the Church was faithfully reflected in that of her successor Paul I. In an imperial decree regulating succession, he casually stated that "the Russian sovereigns are the heads of the Church," a statement which could scarcely have startled an establishment which had

[1] J. S. Curtis, *Church and State in Russia* (New York: Columbia University Press), p. 27.

experienced the reforms of Peter I and Catherine II and did no more than to make explicit the claims of the Ecclesiastical Instructions. More important was the fact that Paul gave substance to his theory by subordinating the Synod to the Senate and the High Procurator to the Procurator General, in making liberal use of the provisions of a decree issued by Catherine that other officials besides the High Procurator might be used as intermediaries between the Synod and the tsar, in keeping close watch and issuing frequent instructions to the Synod, and in instituting the significant custom that the High Procurator's reports on synodal business should not be presented to him directly but sent to the Secretary of State. The effect of all this was to extend and strengthen the hold of the bureaucracy on the hierarchy.

The unstable temperament and vacillating disposition of Alexander I was nowhere more apparent than in his religious addictions. Always over-responsive to strong influences in his environment, he was exposed to the intellectual and moral decadence of his father's court and in his youth professed rationalist views in a dilettante manner. Through his association with Baroness von Krüdener he was introduced to a bizarre and emotional variety of Protestantism and was encouraged in this flight by his Secretary of State and High Procurator of the Holy Synod, Prince Alexander Galitzin, for his own more serious purposes. The emperor smiled benevolently on Galitzin's patronage of the Bible Society, an organization which purported to have no other aim than to acquaint Russians more widely with Holy Writ by distributing vernacular translations throughout the land. The translations were, however, tendentious and the inspiration and some of the initial funds came from Protestants abroad. The ecclesiastical authorities viewed with alarm the Society's open encouragement of evangelical Christianity, and its covert league with dissenting sects. The reaction set in when Alexander fell under the sway of Photius, the superior of the Dereviantsky Monastery in Novgorod. Photius was a fanatic and intrigant of the first order and antici- pated many of the more sinister characteristics of Rasputin. He succeeded in completely captivating the tsar, supplanted Galit- zin in the royal favor, and turned the tsar back to the most rigid practice of Orthodoxy.

The period 1824–1917 witnessed the progressive encroach- ment of the High Procuratorship on all departments of eccle- siastical administration. In spite of the sweeping powers con- veyed to the High Procurator by the Ecclesiastical Instructions the earliest incumbents of that office had difficulty in bringing the Holy Synod to a strict observance of the most elementary requirements of the law. The High Procurator found himself blocked at every turn by the stubborn resistance of the Holy Synod to his authority and by the political intrigue of the Privy Council and the Imperial Cabinet. In the reign of Elizabeth Petrovna the High Procurator was permitted official access to the tsarina only through the autocratic General Procurator of the Senate, Prince Trubetskoi. However, the new Procurator, Prince Shachovskoi, was a man of great sagacity and tact and succeeded in ingratiating himself with the empress and in rec- onciling the Synod to the point where they not only admitted his supervision, but accepted his recommendations on such im- portant matters as clerical training and appointments and the religious education of the laity. By a brilliant coup he per- suaded the tsarina to abolish the Senate Finance Committee to which in 1738 the control of Church property and finance had been transferred, but he became at the same time her watchful overseer of the dispensation of Church funds.

Shachovskoi's successors, Lvov and Kozlovskii, lacked the initiative and energy of their predecessor and were less effec- tive in meeting the obstructionist tactics of the Synod. The Finance Committee was revived with full powers by Peter III whose religious policy was presaged by his charming habit as a youth of thumbing his nose at the priests and deacons during divine service. The Great Catherine recognized the inadvisability of this precipitate move and restored to the Church control over its property, but her heart was not in this gesture and after carefully preparing the ground, launched her decree for the sequestration of Church property. This decree made explicit in the most dramatic possible manner her resolve to subordinate the Church to the State. Under such a regime the office of High Procurator was bound to rise in importance and the tsarina felt the need for a more vigorous executive than Kozlovskii, whom she replaced in 1763.

The High Procurators of Catherine's reign were men chosen not only to execute her policies, but to reflect her private ideas on religion and the Church. Chebyshev (1768–74) is said to have professed atheism openly and made no attempt to conceal his contempt for his clerical colleagues in the Synod. The latter ultimately brought about his ruin on a charge of misappropriation of funds. The episode is characteristic of the growing tension between the Synod and the High Procurator.

Catherine's reign saw the rise and fall of nine Procurators. None were men of great distinction; all were defeated by the growing hostility of the Synod to their office and the absence of firm government support. They preserved, however, not only a tension but a balance between the government and the Church and served as a constant reminder to the ecclesiastical authorities that government supervision and intervention, especially in financial matters, was inescapable. In the reign of Paul the situation was complicated by the clash of two forceful personalities, Metropolitan Ambrose and the High Procurator Yakovlev, both of whom had the ear of the tsar. The latter's term extended into the reign of Alexander I and Yakovlev struck a new note and further aggravated his clerical opponents in his advocacy of a new edition of the Scriptures in the vernacular. The plan was blocked and had to wait until Yakovlev's successor, Prince Alexander Galitzin, revived it in connection with the much disputed Bible Society. Even Yakovlev, however, was not resolute enough to please Alexander who wrote in 1803 to Galitzin:

> I would very much like you to take over the post of High Procurator of the Holy Synod. . . . I want a man attached to me and, so to speak, my man to occupy this important office. I never received Yakovlev and never worked with him but you will deal directly with me because I shall at the same time nominate you my State Secretary.

Galitzin's career was in many respects as checkered as Alexander's and like his was complicated by personal eccentricities. The procuratorship seemed to the tsar an inadequate instrument of state control over the Church, and having strengthened Galitzin's hand in numerous ways he made the startling move in 1817 of constituting his adviser Minister of Religious Affairs and Public Education. The procuratorship was taken over by Prince Mescherskii, but this office, together with the Synod under it, lost much of its political significance to the new ministry.

This sudden eclipse of the Synod and procuratorship was only temporary, for the Ministry of Religious Affairs and Public Education proved too unpopular to be maintained. It was abolished by the new ecclesiastical constitution of 1824, but its enlarged control over Church affairs reverted to the High Procurator Mescherskii. The latter functioned as a minister of state personally responsible to the tsar and in the reign of Alexander I was expected to embody his autocratic attitude toward the Synod. In a dispute over a case of prohibited degree in marriage the Synod failed to reach a clear decision and the emperor wrote Mescherskii:

> There can and must be no disagreement on the dogmas of the faith. Therefore I cannot accept such a statement from the highest

spiritual officer in the state. It is your duty to instruct the members of the Synod and when general unanimity of opinion has been reached, based not on theorizings and interpretations but on an exact comprehension of doctrine, then you are to present it to me.

Mescherskii's successor, Nechaev, obtained the right to use the imperial seal on rescripts issuing from his office, and substantially increased his staff of assistants. He proposed to establish residence in the building of the Synod in order to keep a more careful and personal watch over his subordinates, and although this suggestion was rejected by the tsar he was given control over the three departments of ecclesiastical administration: the Synodal Chancellery, the Department of Ecclesiastical Affairs of the Greco-Russian Faith, and the Commission on Theological Education. In this way the machinery of Church administration and finance, the resolution of questions of faith and morals, and the education of the clergy, which to a large degree also meant its selection and the disposition of ecclesiastical careers, became his province. These measures did not pass unchallenged by the Synod to whose members they were in the highest degree irritating and humiliating. The Metropolitan of Moscow, Philaret, warned of the dangers of too Roman a discipline for the Russian Church.

High hopes for the return of a larger measure of clerical autonomy were entertained of Nechaev's successor, Count Protasov, a man noted for his piety and devotion to the Church. The Synod's enthusiasm was, however, premature and short-lived, for Protasov carried forward vigorously Nechaev's policy of absorbing more and more detailed control over Church administration than his predecessor and did not hesitate to block his opponents and increase his jurisdiction by covert appeals to the secular authorities. The Synod was resentful but powerless in the face of the tsar's support of the Procurator.

Under Nechaev and Protasov the clergy became a bureaucracy within a bureaucracy and always the underdog. In prac-

tice they had recourse to the tsar only through the High Procurator who exercised a strict supervision of the political and
social sympathies of the higher clergy and, through his agents
and inspectors of parochial and educational affairs and the
secret police, of the lower clergy as well. Espionage became an
accepted instrument and suspicion a normal attitude of mind.
The climax of this system was reached in the long procuratorship of Pobedonostsev (1880–1905), a man of narrow and rigid
views, a ruthless administrator and disciplinarian, and an in-
transigent imperialist who opposed with great force and single-
ness of purpose every liberal tendency in Russia. More than
any other person at the court of Nicholas II, more than the unstable tsar or the obtuse and autocratic tsarina, Pobedonostsev
succeeded in convincing the majority of liberals and intellectuals of the hopelessness of reform and in persuading the revolutionaries of the indispensability of violence.

In a real sense Pobedonostsev and Rasputin were inevitable
products of the same system, incurable symptoms of the same
disease. Both were extreme examples, Rasputin of the decadence of piety divorced from enlightened conviction, Pobedonostsev of an absolutism fearful for its strength yet blind to its
most telling defects. That the last empress should fall victim to
the one, the last emperor to the other, is one of the most dramatic ironies of history.

At the outbreak of the revolution in 1917 the Church in its
official policy epitomized and symbolized all that the liberals
and radicals most disliked in the imperial system. It was autocratic and repressive and served as the state's chief support in
maintaining the most backward social system west of the Turk-
ish Empire. All education under its control was limited in
scope, tendentious in aim and sterile in result. Secular education of a high order existed in Russia in spite of the Church,
not because of it; in this respect the hopes and projects of
Peter I and Prokopovich had failed of realization. The ideas of

the *Aufklärung* and the scientific developments of the eighteenth and nineteenth centuries had their counterparts in Russia, and universities and academies occupied a strong though hardly won position. But their most fanatical opponents and most watchful critics were the clergy and the reactionary statesmen who pulled the strings of the puppet hierarchy.

The failure of the Church to solve or contribute to the solution of any of the problems which precipitated the crisis of revolution was in reality the failure of the tsarist state which, having subjected the Church to its control, failed utterly to understand the real function of religion in society, the nature and legitimate scope of its social action, its irrepressible autonomy, and its inviolable integrity.

The effect of government control upon the Church was to denature and pervert its spiritual influence. It was compelled by leaders less wise and less far-seeing than Peter I, who first shackled it to the wheels of the machinery of state, to cultivate a piety irreconcilable with the knowledge and at variance with the aspirations of the time. Not for the first time in history an informed secular moral sense outstripped the dictates of consciences warped rather than quickened by religion, and when the test came not only the Church's outer defenses but its inner resistance crumbled. The fabric of its devotion was worn and brittle. Especially in the large towns, among the workers and in the army, among people uprooted from their native soil and exposed to novel and exciting influences was this the case. The lamp before the icon flickered and paled in the glowing fires of revolution. The droning voices of the priests were shouted down by the strident cries of the leaders of a new era.

Chapter II

RUSSIAN DISSENT

THE FIRST PLANK IN THE BOLSHEVIK PLAT-
form was to attack and fatally weaken the Orthodox Church
in Russia. In the Communist view imperialism and Orthodoxy
were too closely interlocked and their social action too concerted to permit of separation. The ideology and social pattern
of the Church had been antirevolutionary before 1917; it was
certain to be counterrevolutionary thereafter. The Orthodox
Church, however, did not contain all religious persons in Russia. In spite of persecution, civil disabilities, and the activities of
the High Procurator and the imperial police, Russian dissent
survived and in a measure flourished. The policy of the Bolsheviks toward it was based on a simple strategy. As long as
the Orthodox Church was a power and embodied a tendency
to cling or return to the imperial regime the revolutionaries
were prepared to encourage the sects, for the latter were in
principle hostile to the imperial Church and their diversity assisted in the decentralization of religious organizations and the
enervation of religion as a social force. This encouragement
was, however, a purely temporary expedient. As soon as the
power of the Orthodox Church was broken the Revolution
must turn its attack on the sects, for these were identified with
the interests of the bourgeoise just as definitely as Orthodoxy
supported the rule of the tsars. All religion was in Marx's
phrase "the people's opium" and this drug must be taken off

the market. This, however, could best be done in two stages: first eliminate the massive traffic of the established Church and then proceed to clean up the small peddlers and their less well-fortified centers of distribution.

The position of dissent in Russia was a peculiar one, its history quite different from that of Western Protestantism, and its understanding is more likely to be obscured than clarified by European analogies. In view of the rigidly autocratic system of government in Russia, the degree of tolerance accorded to other religions than that of the established Church has been remarkable. Even before Peter I this was the case, and although his decree on freedom of conscience was influenced by Western liberalism, it stands in the main line of Russian tradition. Naturally this toleration did not extend to rivalry with the Orthodox Church. It was primarily a measure of courtesy toward foreigners whose presence in great numbers was essential to Peter's reforms. It did not include an easy tolerance of native schismatic sects or of moves by Roman Catholics and Protestants to convert Orthodox subjects of the tsar and so weaken the establishment.

Apart from the Orthodox Church, Christianity in Russia falls into three main categories: (1) Roman Catholicism which infiltrated into Russia mainly from Poland and was spread by the vigorous propaganda of the religious orders, notably the Jesuits and Dominicans; (2) Protestantism which was brought to Russia from Germany in the sixteenth and seventeenth centuries and from France and Holland in the eighteenth century by persons visiting or residing permanently in Russia for business or political reasons; and (3) the native Russian dissenting sects of which the largest and most important was that of the Old Believers, but which included a wide variety both of homely, pietistic and of mystical and exotic movements.

1. It was inevitable that Rome should cast a wistful eye on Slavic Christianity and make sporadic attempts to repair her

diplomatic blunders in dealing with Slavic countries. Bulgaria was lost in the ninth century through Pope Nicholas I's lack of vision in refusing to grant that kingdom a metropolitan of its own. Once established, Byzantium kept its hold on the Eastern Balkans, dominating the cultural life of Bulgaria from the ninth to eleventh centuries and of Serbia from the eleventh to thirteenth centuries, and emerging as the dominant religion of the Russian states, Kiev, Novgorod, and Moscow. The rise of the Moscow state was not favorable to Rome and no serious efforts were made to alter this situation until the sixteenth century.

The appearance of Protestants in Russia at the time of the Reformation and the tolerance accorded them there opened the eyes of the Vatican to new possibilities. The opportunity seemed made for the newly founded Society of Jesus whose missionary zeal and opposition to Protestant advance were challenged by the prospects in Russia.

With the support of the Austrian emperor the Jesuits began missionary work in Moscow at the end of the seventeenth century and established a house and a school. This first attempt, however, lasted only a year or so and they were expelled at the insistence of the Patriarch Joachim (1688). They had, however, powerful friends at court, notably Prince Basil Galitzin and General Patrick Gordon and their interests were the special concern of the Austrian ambassador Curzius. In view of the increasing number of Roman Catholic immigrants in Moscow, the government in 1681 permitted one priest (who might not be a Jesuit) to reside there and Curzius succeeded in getting him a curate, a Dominican attached to the Austrian embassy. From this modest beginning, Rome launched a campaign of proselytism. In 1692 Father Bleer, O.P. arrived in Moscow with two missionaries and these were followed five years later by others, always with the covert support of Austria and under the eye of General Gordon. They built a small chapel on property owned by an Italian Guasconi whose house had served earlier as a center of Jesuit activity and who was suspected of being a crypto-Jesuit himself. The matter was reported to Peter I, who ordered the work stopped but actually winked at the project out of regard to his favorite general. Before the close of the century, the Jesuits had begun to reappear, some as *soi-disant* missionaries to India and Persia, others as confessors attached to the Austrian embassy. They received a grant of 800 thalers a year from the tsar, opened churches with schools for Russian children in Moscow and St. Petersburg, and persuaded the Minister of Foreign Affairs to send them students preparing for diplomatic careers. Relations between Austria and Russia were strained by the negotiations for the extradition of the tsarevich Alexis, and the Jesuits suffered as objects of Austrian patronage and were again expelled from the country, April 17, 1719.

For Peter I, however, the Jesuits were a special case and Catholics as a whole enjoyed complete freedom in the practice of their religion and extended their propaganda as far south and east as Astrakhan. By a decree of the Holy Synod in 1721 marriages with Catholics were allowed, provided they did not serve as an excuse for proselytizing. For a brief period the Franciscans and Carthusians became the Jesuits' successors, but like the former their missionary zeal overran their discretion and they too were expelled in 1724 to be succeeded by the Dominicans.

The abortive negotiations between Peter I and the Sorbonne were followed by a second attempt by the French theologians to effect reunion between Moscow and Rome. The agent selected was the Abbé Jubet who came to Moscow as private tutor of the children of Princess Irene Dolgaroukov, but his real mission soon became apparent and he was expelled from Russia in 1732.

In 1730 proselytism by Roman clergy was prohibited by law

but the decree had only a limited effect. This was in large part due to the acuteness of the Polish question in the reign of Catherine the Great. After the partition of Poland large territories in which Roman Catholicism was the prevailing religion, passed into Russian hands. Tolerance and wise statesmanship were required to meet this problem. With characteristic insight and firmness Catherine adopted a policy of toleration in all matters affecting the practice of religion among her new subjects. In ecclesiastical administration, however, she perceived the innumerable possibilities of social and political influence from Rome and through Rome from the foreign powers associated with her. Her policy was, therefore, to establish a strong Roman hierarchy politically loyal to herself and to force upon it such measure of autonomy as to render it as far as possible free from Roman direction in local affairs. In 1772 she ordered that no papal bulls or instructions might be published or communicated to the faithful without the permission of the Russian government.

The most effective collaborator in her scheme was Bishop Siestrzencewicz, canon of Wilno, whose great abilities she recognized and whom she resolved to make her representative in the management of Roman Catholic affairs. Siestrzencewicz was a man of integrity and sagacity, cultivated and liberal and with a remarkable talent for reconciling the interests of his Church with the requirements of his sovereign. His program of education and reform was strikingly like the recommendations of the Ecclesiastical Instructions and similarly inspired by the ideas of the *Aufklärung*. He saw as clearly as Catherine the danger of Roman ecclesiastics playing politics in Russia and upheld the sovereign rights of bishops in their own dioceses. Roman bishops, like the Orthodox, had authority over all matters monastic and secular, and the Orders were forbidden to receive and act on orders from their superiors at Rome or from the Pope. Siestrzencewicz proposed the establishment of an ecclesiastical college for the management of Catholic affairs with a High Procurator to represent the crown. In 1797 legal jurisdiction over the Roman hierarchy was assigned to the special department of the Ministry of Justice and in 1798 this department was put under the archbishop, whose wide and extraordinary powers were protected by Paul I in the face of great dissatisfaction expressed by the papal nuncio.

It is not surprising that a man of this type should excite the opposition of the Jesuits who saw in his liberalism and ready acceptance and exercise of more than Gallican privileges a formidable obstacle to their own designs. They therefore resolved upon the metropolitan's ruin. A certain Father Gruber was dispatched to the court of Paul. He was a man of great personal force and charm and was particularly well versed in natural science. With the help of the Catholic coteries in Moscow and St. Petersburg he met the tsar upon whom he made a most favorable impression. Before long Father Gruber had the exceptional privilege of free entry to the tsar's presence at all times. Needless to say, this friendship was not disadvantageous to the Society. The Church at St. Petersburg was returned to them with all its endowments, a school and seminary were opened, and estates confiscated in 1773 were restored. More important, however, than these concessions was Father Gruber's success in poisoning the tsar's mind against the metropolitan. Siestrzencewicz was arrested and banished to his estates where he remained in exile until the succession of Alexander I, when the Jesuits again lost favor. He was recalled in 1801 and restored to his former dignities. Shortly before his return the ecclesiastical college which he had recommended was established to replace the old legal department and the archbishop was made its first president. Father Gruber lost his prestige and in spite of the support of Prince Galitzin and a number of high-ranking converts among the ladies of the court, the Society which had for so many years enjoyed the singular protection of a government which did not even share its faith, was expelled from Russia in 1815. The decree of banishment drawn up by Admiral Shishkoff described the divisive and unsettling influence of the Jesuits in Russia in biting words. Provided by the government with fur coats and winter boots for the journey, they were escorted to Polotsk by the imperial police. Count Maistre, blandly disregarding the singular favor they had enjoyed in Russia since the time of Catherine, described them as "a battalion banished on account of its valor."

The Jesuits were succeeded by the Dominicans who did little to restore the confidence of the government in the Russian hierarchy, so shaken by the Jesuits. The metropolitan was no longer young and vigorous and his opponents in the new ecclesiastical college made it as difficult as possible for him to exercise his rights, to immunize the Russian hierarchy from outside interference in administration, and to keep the religious orders from receiving and acting on instructions from abroad. There was constant conflict between Roman canon and Russian civil law, and the latter was by no means always respected. The seminary at Wilno offered admirable education in both the sciences and humanities but was opposed by the reactionary clergy led by the Dominicans and its work severely hampered. In 1801 the long struggle over the right of clerical appointments was unwisely decided in favor of Roman canon law. Livings were obtained largely by preferment and episcopal sanction degenerated into a mere formality. The intellectual and moral conditions of the priests which Siestrzencewicz had tried so hard to elevate sank to a level as low, if not lower, than that of the Orthodox. Conditions in the monasteries were no better and relations between the different orders and between the religious and secular clergy contained all these elements of dissension and rivalry which Catherine and her adviser had sought to obviate.

The history of diplomatic relations between Russia and the Vatican in the nineteenth and early twentieth centuries involved no new problems, but rather a constant and never wholly satisfactory reworking of old ones. The perennial attraction of the Roman Church in all countries requires no special explanation in Russia: its orderliness and discipline of mind and life appealed to some temperaments as an attractive alternative to the fluidity of the Orthodox dogmatic tradition, the chaotic state of its clerical administration, and the confusion arising from its exploitation by the state. Catholic social policy was conservative and its appeal was felt in all strata of society, though rather more at the top than at the bottom and in the large cities rather than in the small towns and countryside. Count Maistre wrote enthusiastically in 1816, "Conversions to our faith are very rapid and proselytism to Catholicism strikes one as much by the number of persons as by the rank they occupy in society. It is truly an admirable sight, as most of these conversions are principally among the first orders of society." Except in areas taken over by the partition of Poland and in the Ukraine, conversion to Rome detached the convert from the political currents of the established Church. It was therefore not the vehicle of class sentiments or economic interests. In the ideology and mobilization of the Revolution it was a negligible factor.

2. The arrival of Protestantism in Russia was not due, in the first instance, to any missionary zeal on the part of Western Europeans nor to any demand for a reformation along the lines of Luther and Calvin within the Orthodox Church. It was imported by foreign residents who were allowed freedom in the practice of their religion, as they were permitted the use of their own speech and manner of dress. Like Roman Catholics they were not allowed to proselytize and not even mixed marriages could be used as an excuse for conversions. In such cases

the Orthodox partner and the children must remain Orthodox; the Protestant husband or wife might, but need not, accept Orthodoxy.

In 1575 there was a Lutheran community established in Moscow with its own pastor and place of worship, and its members grew so rapidly that imperial permission was granted early in the seventeenth century to build a new church. Boris Godunov contributed a bell tower with three bells. Not much later, a congregation of Dutch Reformed was set up in Moscow and for a time shared with the Lutherans the use of their church building. German military officers and technicians employed by Peter I formed a Lutheran congregation at St. Petersburg and at the request of Vice-Admiral Cruys were permitted to call its pastor, Wilhelm Tolle, from Amsterdam in 1704. Similar foundations arose in Kronstadt, on the island of Vasili-Ostrov near St. Petersburg, in Astrakhan, at Barnaul in Siberia, and in Archangel. Peter's Swedish campaign added a large number of Swedish and Finnish Lutherans to his subjects. Members of the Swedish, Finnish congregations of Nymschanz and Narva were deported to St. Petersburg and employed as laborers and domestics and formed the first Lutheran congregation there, antedating by a brief period the German Lutherans who were voluntary immigrants. The large number of German mercenary troops, staffed with German officers, occasioned the appointment of German army chaplains and secured the new congregations influential patrons at court. The Imperial Landcadettencorps at St. Petersburg was supplied with a chapel and chaplain by the Tsarina Anna Ivanovna at the instigation of von Münnich. The congregation at St. Petersburg early established a school, the curriculum of which was so comprehensive and the instruction so thorough that it attracted Russian as well as German students. Unlike the Roman Catholics the Lutherans appear scrupulously to have avoided using these privileges as opportunities for gaining converts to their faith.

In the administration of spiritual matters the Protestant congregations were autonomous. Peter I appointed one of the Lutheran pastors in 1711 as Superintendent with power to govern the Church and the responsibility for maintaining order in it, and this appointment was confirmed by an imperial decree in 1715. In 1723 Lutherans and Reformed were allowed to build churches and schools in all parts of the empire. Projects for the rebuilding of churches and for the erection of new churches and schools often enjoyed the liberal patronage of the tsars who on more than one occasion contributed amounts up to 1,000 rubles.

In questions involving both civil rights and ecclesiastical privileges, Protestants came under the combined jurisdiction of their own governing bodies and the College of Justice. The former was presided over by a "Patron" chosen from one of the high-ranking German officers or diplomats at the court. A tendency on the part of the College of Justice to ignore the rights of the clergy met with successful resistance in the reign of Anna Ivanovna. Matters falling under this jurisdiction involved not only the formalities attendant on marriage, births, baptisms, and deaths but also marriage disputes, illegitimacy, and moral dereliction. Something in the atmosphere of the Russian capital appears to have affected the susceptibilities of the resident foreigners, for a large proportion of the cases cited by Büsching involve sins of the flesh. One unfortunate widow so far abandoned herself to frivolity that she was denounced by the Kirchenrat, *als . . . ein rechter Schandfleck unserer evangelischen Gemeinde.* The severity of this condemnation is ample indication that the moral fibre of the congregation as a whole was unaffected by the sporadic lapses of its members.

The Lutherans by no means held the field alone. Calvinists from Holland and France, Mennonites from Holland, and Baptists whose origins in Russia along with the so-called Stundists, form the transition from imported brands of Protestantism to native sects, were partly inspired, partly reinforced by influences outside Russia. The Baptist movement in Russia began with the spiritual crisis of one Martin Kalweit, a Lutheran, who pressed his zeal so far that he was forced to leave Russia for Germany where he found among the Baptists of that country an understanding of his experience and missionary aims. He returned to Russia via the Caucasus where he picked up some followers and began to propagate his ideas and form congregations. Not unnaturally this contravention of the law against proselytizing aroused the opposition of the Orthodox clergy and the Baptists were forced to lead a half-concealed existence, supported materially and morally by their brethren in England and America.

3. The history of the native Russian dissident sects has yet to be written, although many valuable special studies have been made. The best account of them in English is by the late F. W. Conybeare, who wrote in the preface to his *Russian Dissenters,* "I trust that my work may be of some use to those who sincerely desire to understand and trace out the springs of the Revolution." The Russian sects, however, had little effect on the events of 1917 and after. They were neither hotbeds of sedition nor reliable guardians of conservatism. The social attitudes of the different groups varied considerably and form no single, unified social pattern. The Old Believers were die-hards in liturgics and theology and were convinced not only that the old time religion was good enough for them, but that every accretion and fortuitous error that had become accepted and standardized was sacrosanct. Although the controversy with the Patriarch Nikon began over the correction of the service books, it revealed a stubborn conservatism of mind which was equally unyielding in matters of theology and social sympathy.

The Tolstoyans, in spite of their passive disobedience to the state and disdain of the world, were Quietists and lacked social initiative. Their influence began with the individual and ended in small self-contained communities. The exotic sects, like the Chlystii and Skoptsi with their strange doctrines and asocial practices, offered an insecure retreat for the emotionally unstable but contributed nothing distinctive to Russian social life as a whole.

Probably the most important of these sects sociologically were those whose ethos most closely resembled that of Western Protestantism and who co-operated complacently with its followers in Russia. Notable among these were the Molokanye, the Dukhobors, the Adventists and the Stundists.

The Stundists were a pietistic group which emerged, rather like Methodism in its early phase, in the established Church but through contact with the Baptists acquired a form of their own and became an independent sect. They derived their name, also like the Methodists, from their peculiar devotional practices. *Stunda* is the German *Stunde* and refers to the hours set aside for prayer and Bible reading by small groups or congregations. As a movement Stundism arose early in the eighteenth century but it became a sect, separate from Orthodoxy and with rites of its own about 1870. It was strongest in the Caucasus and South Russia where it coalesced not only with imported Protestant sects but with the persecuted remnants of native dissenters like the Molokanye and Dukhobors.

The tendency on the part of Russia nonconformists to intermingle in worship and fraternal association and to minimize their individual differences in theology and cult is observable even in the seventeenth century. Regardless of origins the drift of Russian dissent (apart from the Old Believers) was toward a Protestant emphasis on the Bible as the sole authority in belief, on a gripping personal experience of conversion, and on interior illumination and guidance.

An interesting example of this is found in the autobiography of a convert to Stundism, A. I. Stefanovich.[1] This man was born in 1861, the son of an Orthodox priest in the Chersonese, and as the eldest son it was naturally assumed that he would follow in his father's profession. He received his elementary education from an uncle who, though a priest, was infected with Stundist notions, knew German and was a close friend of the German evangelical pastor of the district. He was impatient of the duties of his office, despised the Church ceremonies which he treated with indifference and once remarked, "In my opinion the Stundists are good people. In any case they are not so stupid as we, who have turned our worship into idolatry." He described clerical vestments as "a cloak for evil" and was so prejudiced against monasticism that he used to order any religious who ventured to call on him to be chased with a stick.

Another uncle who was a priest was less antagonistic to his own Church, but was also infected with Stundism. An observation of his recalled by Stefanovich reveals how eclectic theology in such circles could become:

Stundism is true Christianity. If the Stundists read the pure gospel and believe in salvation through Jesus and a change for the better is observable in their life, it is clear that they are on the right track. Christ is the Centre. We Greek Catholics are not far from the periphery. If the Stundists are near the Centre, they must be more illuminated by the Sun. He who walks in the Sun, will be illuminated by it.

In accordance with the wishes of the first-mentioned uncle and rather against those of his remote and conventional father, the boy was sent to the gymnasium and later to the theological school in Odessa. Here he not only pursued his course with success but took full advantage of surreptitious access to books on science, philosophy, and sociology. They so contrasted with

[1] *"Aus der Arbeit unter den Stundisten," Hefte zum christlichen Orient,* 3. Berlin, 1904.

the narrow mentality of his professors and the ascetic discipline of school life that they roused in him great animosity to
Orthodoxy. As in many seminaries of the period liberal political ideas were current among the students.

At the end of his course he returned home completely opposed to a clerical career. In an interview with his father he
declared passionately, "I do not believe in any God or in any
spiritual reality. Besides I hate your religion and cannot understand how an intelligent and educated man can have faith at
all. How can you ask me to become a priest?" To this outburst
his father made the reply, "It doesn't matter that you believe
nothing. Many priests believe in neither God nor devil but
serve Holy Church faithfully. This is a question of your liveli-
hood." Stefanovich persisted in his refusal and left his father's
house to enter military service. Upon the discovery of his connection with a politically liberal group he was forced to leave
Russia and joined the Bulgarian army.

In Sofia Stefanovich had rooms in the house of a pious
Protestant woman and made the acquaintance of a pastor employed by the Congregationalist Mission, an able theologian and
doctor of medicine. Under these influences he began to attend
the services of the Evangelical Church, and after hearing a
particularly impressive sermon there was converted with the
usual inner crisis. His piety greatly increased and was observed
by his fellow officers and superiors who regarded this addiction
as a lamentable eccentricity and as conduct unbecoming an
officer and a gentleman. He was ultimately forced to resign his
commission and gave himself up wholly to the work of an
evangelist and missionary. He learned English in order to read
Protestant theology in that language and worked in the well-
stocked library of a Bulgarian Protestant pastor.

In 1894 he returned to Russia to visit his parents. He was
amiably received but his father forbade him to associate with
Stundists, threatening him with the police. He managed, how-

ever, to establish such connections secretly with the help of a local police officer. In 1899 he became a regular associate of the German Mission to the East. In 1900 he visited St. Petersburg where he preached to congregations of two to three thousand Russian Baptists. At this time there were forty such groups, two of which were recognized by the government. They had formerly been divided among themselves by a freer or stricter adherence to doctrine but this difference lost its importance in time. Stefanovich reports visits to a number of strange sects in the country: for example, the Chichuli who confessed their sins before the congregation and received its absolution, and the Skritniti who lived in caves and sought the Truth in inner experience. The latter lived so withdrawn a life that when one of its members was impelled to seek the Truth in St. Petersburg and met a cow at an early stage of his journey, he hastened back to his cave convinced that he had seen the beast of the Apocalypse and that the Day of Judgment had arrived. In spite of differences of view Stefanovich was received in a friendly spirit by all these groups and preached to them his own message. The sense of a common lot and common religious aim in Russian dissent led to correspondence with evangelical brethren abroad on questions of organization and doctrine.

This interchange between the sects was reflected in the attitude of the government toward them. In Odessa, Stefanovich reports the Baptists and the Freibrüder kept apart but the government called all sects in south Russia "Stundists" and treated them as such. They were suspected by the local population of being German agents preparing the way for the Kaiser's conquests. For this, as well as for religious reasons, they were mercilessly persecuted. Not only the government, but unauthorized groups of fanatics hunted them down and subjected them to the most brutal tortures.

An even more remarkable career than that of Stefanovich is that of I. S. Prokhanov, the founder of the All-Russian

Evangelical Christian Union. Prokhanov was born in 1869 of Molokanye parents in a small village of the Caucasus. At seventeen he experienced conversion but continued his secular studies and became an engineer. Like Stefanovich he read German philosophy and passed through a period of skepticism. In 1887 he joined the Baptist congregation in his native village of Vladikavkas.

The assassination of Alexander II was a blow to liberal religious policy and his successor, under the influence of such reactionary absolutists as Pobedonostsev, outlawed Stundism and initiated a reign of terror among dissenters. Prison and exile were not unusual. The dissenters, however, contrived to meet in secret, often aided by sympathetic government agents. In the face of opposition Prokhanov continued his work as lay missionary and founded a religious monthly, *Besseda,* which circulated privately with great effect. Shortly after graduating from the Technical Institute at St. Petersburg, he visited L. Tolstoy and was invited to read the author's manuscript of *The Kingdom of God,* but was not impressed. He said:

I admired him for his great literary ability and his writings on the moral phase of Christianity but I could not follow him as a religious teacher, because he really misunderstood Christ, throwing away nearly all of the Bible, entirely overlooking the problem of sin and rejecting the necessities of conversion, faith, and prayer —the cardinal elements of the spiritual life.

After some trouble with the police Prokhanov went abroad and with the help of a pious American family in St. Petersburg and a Finnish pastor reached England via Helsingfors, Stockholm, Hamburg, and Paris, always assisted by evangelical friends. With the help of Mr. Brooks, a Quaker, he attended the Baptist College in Bristol and the New Congregational College in London. Later he studied at the University of Berlin and with the Faculté de Théologie Protestante in Paris. In

1898 he went to Cyprus to minister to a colony of exiled Dukhobors and thence returned to Russia where he worked first in his native village, later in Riga and St. Petersburg.

In 1905 the government issued an Act of Toleration as a concession to the revolutionary demands of the people. A contributing factor was a report to the Ministry of the Interior by Prokhanov. Lenin commented distrustfully on the role of the dissenters in this brief period of liberation, and Pobedonostsev did his best to offset their gains by founding a missionary society which was in effect an organization of clerical spies designed to discover and mark out for exile all Protestant leaders. The principal advantage in the new Act was that it permitted the Evangelicals freedom to publish religious and devotional books. In 1906 the first Duma allowed schismatics "to organize congregations and churches and to develop their activities," and this policy was in general supported by the Ministry of the Interior's Department for Religious Affairs and by the Duma's Commission on Religious Cults which was headed by the pro-Protestant Kaunusky. In 1909 the All-Russian Evangelical Christian Union was founded and Prokhanov elected president. Missionary work flourished and a congregation of one thousand met in the Terishevsky Hall in St. Petersburg. In 1913 the first Protestant theological school was opened in that city. The war (1914–18) served as an excuse to restrict evangelical liberties; religious publications were suppressed, conferences and even meetings were forbidden, the Bible school was closed, and Prokhanov was arrested as a revolutionary.

The Kerensky government gave promise of a new era of liberation. Publications and meetings were resumed and a small political party was started, the Christian Democrats. All this was, however, swept away in the October revolution. At first the government appeared to favor the sects in accordance with the policy enunciated by Lenin in 1905. In spite of danger and hardships Prokhanov remained in Leningrad directing what was left of the evangelical work there and corresponding with congregations throughout Russia. Before it was forbidden he succeeded in importing fifty thousand Russian Bibles and New Testaments from abroad, and in 1918 and 1919 held the usual conferences and in 1920 held a joint conference with the Baptists. Seeing their chance in the policy of the Soviets to grant land to small associations, a number of evangelical collectives were formed, received grants of land, established small societies and enjoyed religious freedom under the law. Prokhanov wisely drew up a manual of legal enactments on religion and issued it under the title *Republic and Religion.* In 1921, when things were at their worst, the All-Russian Conference of Christian Young People met in Tver where food conditions were less desperate than in Leningrad and Moscow. One of the meetings was raided by the Cheka and all present were arrested. To the order of arrest Prokhanov replied by turning to the congregation and saying, "Let us pray," and the police, somewhat disconcerted, stood by with leveled revolvers while the congregation joined in prayer. They then marched to the police station singing hymns and continued their conference in jail. After three weeks, twelve of the senior members of the group were sentenced to hard labor at the Suzdal Monastery. Fortunately their treatment there was relatively mild and they were allowed a room for religious meetings.

The conclusion of this episode is instructive of the crosscurrents operating at this time. It transpired that the Cheka had intervened at the instigation of one of its members who was also an Orthodox priest and violently opposed to Protestantism. He had charged that Prokhanov was a counterrevolutionary and was spreading the seeds of reaction through the evangelical groups. The case was reviewed by the Central Committee of Deputies, Workmen and Peasants in Moscow and the falsity of the charges exposed. As Prokhanov and his friends left their prison they met their delator on his way in. He served a term of precisely the length to which his victims had been subjected.

On his return to Leningrad in 1922 Prokhanov called a meeting of the All-Russian Evangelical Christian Union and set about repairing churches and securing permission for services. In this period of distress the different groups were drawn more closely together, and Prokhanov served them all, preaching most frequently in the Swedish Lutheran and French Reformed Churches. The Bible school was reopened in October, 1922.

In the period of extreme confusion in the Orthodox Church when the patriarch had been induced to abdicate his functions and Krasnitskii, Vvedenskii, and Antonin were peddling their private brands of Orthodoxy with the help and to the great delight of the Soviet unbelievers, Prokhanov felt that the time had come to issue an appeal for reformation and union between the disintegrating factions of Orthodoxy and the dissident bodies. One hundred thousand copies of this appeal were sent out and roused some response in Orthodox circles. The Metropolitan Antonin and some Orthodox clergy were impressed and a certain rapport was established between Orthodoxy and dissent. The Church of Peter and Paul in Moscow was lent to the Evangelicals for their services. In March, 1923 Prokhanov was invited to address the Congress of the Ancient Apostolic Church, was greeted warmly by Vvedenskii and led a large assembly of Orthodox clergy and laity in prayer.

A brief period of imprisonment in the spring of 1923 was followed by six years of happy and productive work facilitated by the government which, at this time, was most actively fostering dissent as a means to its own ends. A hurried trip to America enlisted generous support for publications and missionary work, the former gladly undertaken for a consideration by the presses of the Atheistical Society. In 1926 a week's session of the Christian Conference was held in Leningrad. Preaching missions followed in many smaller cities, in Siberia and the

Caucasus, to workers in the factories, and to peasants in the country.

In 1926 Prokhanov wrote a programmatic statement of the aims of Evangelical Christianity which was adopted at the Conference of that year. It is an interesting disclosure of the social policy of Russian dissent at this time: (1) Every Evangelical Christian should be an example of his faith "not only in his personal behavior but in his conduct in family, social, business and educational life." (2) His conduct must be based on the teaching of Jesus. (3) "Evangelical Christians must acquire all the scientific knowledge possible, either for themselves or their children and take part in the development and extension of scientific achievements. There should not be among us even one illiterate man or woman. All members, both parents and children, must try to secure the highest education commensurate with their means." (4) "The Gospel must find expression in the development of the arts, such as literature, music, architecture, printing, and sculpture." (5) Evangelical Christians must further the government's efforts to improve industry and agriculture by their own efforts in these fields. (6) Christian homes should be beautiful as well as holy. Gardens should be carefully planned and flowers should abound. (7) "Marriage between Evangelical Christians should take place at an early date." (8) Alcohol in all forms should be abjured. (9) Concern for the national welfare of fellow Christians must be a common responsibility.

The interesting feature in this program is its secular emphasis. Prokhanov's scientific training and broad education in many lands came into their own here. More important strategically, however, is the parallelism between the Evangelical program and the contemporary Soviet ideal of self-cultivation, scientific knowledge, social responsibility, and mutual consideration. The "home and garden" touch is as clearly a leaf out of the Soviet book, as the prohibition of alcohol is a survival of Protestant asceticism. Even the recommendation of early marriages sounds a timely note. It is a reply to the early Soviet hostility to the family as an institution and a gentle reminder that the Christian race has every intention both of safeguarding its youth and maintaining its existence.

The Soviet criticism of Russian dissent as a social force is derived mainly from Lenin's writings of 1905–7. The burden of this complaint was that the record of the dissenting sects had been consistently antirevolutionary. They had done nothing to help in the class struggle and in fact had impeded it. The only weapons they were willing to employ against oppression was an innocuous propaganda based on unconvincing platitudes. At the time of the January uprisings (1905) and during the interlude of Stolypin's reforms, they showed themselves credulous of the government's good faith and abject in currying imperial favor. When the proletarian revolution broke and engulfed Russia in a seething tide, it owed nothing to the initiative of the dissenters whose sole value had been as pawns in a game of power politics the grand strategy of which lay far beyond their vision and capacities.

The evidence for thesis has been marshaled by F. M. Putintsev in his work *The Political Role and Tactics of the Sects* (in Russian). Putintsev points out that at the sectarian religious congresses of 1905–7 vigorous protest was made against revolutionary action and unequivocal loyalty to the tsar and his government enjoined. The sectarians identified themselves politically with the liberal-monarchist *bourgeoisie*.

Even at the height of the revolution 1905–7, there were no armed uprisings against the landlords or officials of the imperial government on farms and in villages where sectarians were settled. In the eyes of the liberal *bourgeoisie* all this constituted a favorable contrast in sectarian religion with Orthodoxy. The bourgeois inquisitors could not reproach the sectarians with any sort of socialist sympathies. The top leaders of the sects be they Old Believers, Molokanye, Baptists, Evangelicals, Mennonites, Skoptsi or whatever, were drawn for the most part from the respectable merchant class and even from the nobility. . . . Naturally no one ever thought of accusing such persons of political disloyalty. When 1905 came, the sectarian leaders and the rich "brethren" showed their fidelity. Under the pressure of the revolution the sectarians were promised freedom of conscience, in response to which the sectarian congresses and leaders assured the tsar of their devotion. Especially vocal were the Cadets, the Octobrists, and the "Progressive" clergy among the Old Believers. The Old Believers were at this time in no way dangerous to the Orthodox priests, for cases of conversion from Orthodoxy to the Old Believers were extremely rare. In doctrine and rite the faith of the Old Believers differed but little from that of the Orthodox and former Orthodox priests function in some Old Believers groups to this day, having made the transition to the Old Believers for pay. The "Progressive" clergy (the peaceful reformers), who first made their appearance at that time, stood for freedom of conscience for Old Believers. The Octobrists, in whose number were many prominent Old Believers, were the more favorable to the Old Believers, as they received from them not only moral but financial support, e.g., for the publication of *The Voice of Moscow*. As a result of their activities at this time a whole series of new chapels, especially among the Old Believers, were opened. In 1905 and shortly after, a number of periodicals for Baptists, Evangelicals, Molokanye and some other sects were licensed. Congresses were permitted. Somewhat later the Union of Evangelical Christians was sanctioned. In the period of reaction all these privileges granted to the sects were gradually withdrawn by the imperial government. The latter did not want to "offend" the Orthodox clergy, so the tsar ambiguously declared in his manifestos, "I have granted freedom of religious profession but on condition that the dominant position of the Orthodox Church be maintained and only limited privileges enjoyed by the dissident sects." The sectarians were, however, delighted at these favors granted by the terrified tsar. They followed unreservedly and wholeheartedly their leaders and the latter trailed in the wake of the Octobrist and Cadet Parties.

What did the Octobrists and Cadets want from 1905 up to 1917? They wanted to establish more firmly the power of capital at the cost of a purge of the imperial government and its Church. They demanded from the government and the Church some small innovations in order that both might protect the interest of the *bourgeoisie*. The cumbersome apparatus of bureaucracy in State and Church required, in the view of the Octobrist and Cadets, some small curtailments and improvements. In their opinion the tsar must in some small measure share his power with them and grant a most pathetic, most monarchical constitution and the clergy must share with them their parochial power and agree to independently governed parishes.

Putintsev quotes from communications to the tsar by the congress of Adventists at St. Petersburg in 1905, and from the Baptist congress in London of the same year at which Russian delegates were present, from antirevolutionary writings of the Tolstoyans at this period, from the literature emanating from the one hundredth anniversary of the founding of the Molokanye and the congresses of Old Believers held in 1905–6. An enthusiastic sect known as the New Israelites, an offshoot of the Chlysti, at their congress in 1905, hailed Nicholas as the Tsar Liberator and proposed to institute a new "era of freedom" beginning their calendar with 1905 when the tsar had granted them freedom of worship.

In the period of reaction matters were not improved. Putintsev charges the sectarian leaders with assisting directly and indirectly in the suppression of the revolution of 1905, in the exclusion of the proletariat from political life, and in the exploitation of the masses. Sectarians were among the government's *agents provocateurs* and imperial spies and Baptists acted as jailers in the Peter and Paul fortress prison. The Baptists resolved to serve in the imperial army and in all respects to

obey their superiors and evade none of their military obligations. Obviously recruits for the army of revolution were not to
be found among men of such kidney. The New Israelites went
to the length of deciding not to join any radical party or association. All freedoms in their view should be granted by the tsar
"who had promised to lead them by the way of reform and
enlightenment, not by revolution and bloodshed."

During the great war 1914–17 sectarians served faithfully in
the imperial army in spite of the pacifist propaganda of some
of their leaders and were active in ministering to the wounded
and in keeping up war morale. In an article published in the
Baptist *Word of Truth* (August, 1917, p. 99), its author de-
clares, "We are Russians by nationality; we love our country
and in the ranks of the army are our fathers, brothers, and
children. There are no traitors among the sectarians."

For reasons which are intelligible, but in Putintsev's view
reprehensible, the sectarians found the conditions of the Kerensky regime particularly congenial. The Revolution, however,
shocked them no less than the Orthodox and although they
were not at first the main objective of the Bolshevik campaign
against religion, they had no sympathy with the Communist
creed and still less with its methods. Caught between the devil
and the deep blue sea, they not unnaturally elected to hold their
ground and to remain as aloof as possible from the social conflict going on about them. The theory of pacifism became more
appealing as its practice appeared more timely. A Baptist
minister, the Reverend R. A. Khomyak, published an article in
Slovo Istinny in 1921, in which he said:

Even though the world regard us as traitors, fanatics, unedu-
cated, etc., we must declare categorically, "No, world, I will not go
with you." We will be told, "Where is your patriotism? After all,
ought you not to belong to some political party?" To these questions and pronouncements of the world, we shall briefly and clearly

say, "No, world, we shall not go with you. Our country is the country of Christ; our party is the party of Christ. My kingdom is not of this world."

The Bolsheviks were not slow to observe this change of front from the Baptists' resolution in 1905 to serve loyally in the tsar's army and from the decision of Prokhanov and his friends in 1917 to form a political party under the Provisional Government. It is not surprising that Putintsev complains:

Khomyak was living in Soviet territory, where only the Bolshevik party existed and this was leading the country in a struggle against ruin, and famine, speculation and pillage, bureaucracy and bribery, kulak uprisings and White clergy, typhus and the abandonment of children. In advising the sectaries and all other citizens to keep clear of parties, Khomyak had in mind the Bolshevik party. In advising them not to follow in the way of this present world, Khomyak had in mind Soviet actualities. In advising them to deny their country, Khomyak had in mind the Socialist, Soviet country. Denying the Soviet country meant not to value or defend its achievements. To deny the country of workers and peasants, meant for workers and peasants to betray their vital interests.

It was an additional provocation to the victorious party that those sectaries which did not take a pacifist stand urged membership in the Menshevik party or in one of the more liberal, less radical groups. This sentiment was repeatedly expressed in a series of articles by different authors in the Baptist *Slovo Istinny* in the critical years of 1917–18. One author hesitatingly admitted "that it is not a sin to be a member of the Socialist Revolutionaries, Social Democrats, etc., but happy, happy is the man who is not overwhelmed by them and pursues his own clear vocation." Another, even after the October Revolution and the dissolution of the Constituent Assembly, maintained that it might be permissible for a Christian to vote for one of the "Socialist parties" but never to share in their activities.

Putintsev's accusations of the counterrevolutionary influence of the sects are leveled not only at their ideas and sympathies but also at their acts. It was not difficult to find isolated cases in which sectarians as individuals or groups attempted to avoid the rationing regulations of the lean years of the early twenties. These and similar misdemeanors, including some covert, some active opposition to Bolshevik authority, were occasioned in part by physical need, in part by a lack of enthusiasm or hostility to the current political program, but Bolshevik criticism was right in maintaining that the religious principles of the sectaries encouraged and strengthened these attitudes.

The real onus of the Bolshevik complaint was that all Christian ethics were opposed to revolution and did not permit cooperation in an enterprise the avowed aim of which was to exterminate all religion and inaugurate a godless society. To lend support to this program was religiously quite a different matter from fighting or working for any form of Christian state or any genuinely tolerant state. In this respect Protestant and sectarian sympathies were at one with Orthodoxy and the attack of the Revolution, apart from strategic considerations, was leveled at all religion. The distinction between Orthodoxy and tsarism on the one hand and Dissent and *bourgeoisie* on the other, is part of the Marxian formula but applied much less accurately to Russian than to Western European conditions. In Russia the majority of the *bourgeoisie* were as loyally Orthodox as the nobility and the court. The great industrial magnates as well as the prosperous farmers and small shopkeepers were nearly all members of the established Church. The rise of capitalism and big business did not coincide in Russia with any change in religion as in the West. The attack on Orthodoxy was the real frontal attack on imperialism and *bourgeoisie* alike. The war on the sects was no more than a mopping-up operation in which some bourgeois remnants were liquidated. The difference between their religious principles were negligible and merely served to cover the government's strategy of "divide and rule."

In spite of the stimulus injected into Orthodox theology by the study of Roman Catholic and Protestant divines and the very considerable amount of learning in philosophy and historical theology in the universities and in the theological and secular academies, there was little scope in Russia for a religion of educated men in the European sense of the word. Education of this sort came from abroad and often had to be pursued there, for public instruction was strictly watched and the censorship was extremely sensitive to such tendencies in print. Russian philosophic thought was therefore compelled not only to cross the frontiers of Orthodoxy, but of Russia to find sustenance and acquire a new sense of direction.[2] In the twenties and thirties, however, a new spirit of inquiry had arisen. Hershenson wrote, "It was a time when the word 'philosophy' had in it something magical" and Kirievskii declared, "Philosophy is for us indispensable, our whole intellectual development demands it."

Much of the new spirit was released and fostered by the educational reforms under Alexander I, but Florovskii has pointed out that "the first exponents of philosophical idealism issued from theological seminaries of the period before the reform," and that "it was precisely in the clerical academies that Russian philosophical thought first made contact with German idealism."

Through the universities and theological schools philosophical curiosity was awakened in a whole generation of young men who met often in private circles for discussion, circulated translations of German works in manuscript, and sometimes published in the more liberal periodicals when the hazards of

[2] The following section owes much to G. Florovskii, *Puti Russkavo Bogosloviya*. Paris, 1937.

their existence permitted or wrote pamphlets with limited circulation. These Russian intelligentsia, as they were called, were men drawn from all walks of life, for the most part rationalist and anti-authoritarian in their thinking and so led to place a high value on the individual. They led a common and persistent drive toward a more liberal state of society in which the individual could come into his own and associate on terms of greater equality with his fellows.

The Romantics of the end of the eighteenth century, men like Hertzen and Karamzin, had endowed the rationalists' idol, *Man,* with flesh and blood. They were more concerned with his feelings and wishes than with his abstract "rights," and made him sensible of his homelier contacts with nature and his fellow man. Religious romanticism, however, was a no greater success in Russia than in the West, for in spite of its warmth of feeling it rested on a fundamental misapprehension of religion. Its feebleness is well illustrated in Zhukovski's *Christian Philosophy* (1850). Some of its better characteristics emerge in the poetry of Lermontov whose intense feeling of oneness with nature issued in a religious interpretation of life not unlike Wordsworth's.

The connection between Russian social aspirations and formal philosophic thought was established early in the nineteenth century and survived the shock of 1825. In a sense the Decembrist failure was favorable to the growth of philosophy, for the repressive measures taken by Nicholas I left little scope for reformers and forced liberalism to seek more theoretical outlets. In the first quarter of the century the influence of French rationalism was preponderant, e.g., in Pestel, but Bellanskii, professor of surgery in St. Petersburg, began to expound Schelling in 1805 and a group of young enthusiasts for the new philosophy of nature formed in Moscow under the tutelage of Pavlov. The latter was professor of physics and agriculture who, Hertzen says, "used to stand at the doors of the physico-agricultural department and ask any student the questions, 'You want to know about nature? . . . What is nature? . . . What is learning?'" By 1820 translations of the principal works of Kant, Fichte and Schelling had been completed. Between 1826–40 a series of Russian philosophers, who were in contact with German ideas, appeared on the scene. In Belinskii's striking phrase (1834), "In this decade we [i.e., the Russian intellectuals] felt our way through, thought through and lived through the whole intellectual life of Europe, the echo of which reached us from the Baltic sea." "At the beginning of the nineteenth century," wrote Odoyevskii, "Schelling was what Columbus was in the fifteenth; he opened up to man an unknown portion of his world, his soul, about which only fabulous traditions had hitherto existed." The great appeal of Fichte, Schelling and Hegel, however, lay in their ethical and historical ideas. Kirievskii complained that "readers of Kant stood in a ration of 5 to 5,000 with readers of Schelling," and Belinskii once raged, "You want me to believe that man's goal is to bring the Absolute Spirit to a consciousness of itself and you are content with this role. As for me, I am not such a fool as to serve as anyone's unwilling instrument. If I think, if I suffer, I do so for myself. If your Absolute Spirit exists, he is a stranger to me. I do not wish to make his acquaintance, for I have nothing in common with him."

The effect of the French Revolution and of the ensuing period of unrest in Western Europe was to bring Russian thought closer to the actualities of social change. Reform was no longer an idea but an incipient program, and in every program was latent the germ of revolution. The time was not ripe for action as was shown by the pitiful fiasco of the Decembrist insurrection (1825), but young heads were full of schemes and plans. Pestel, one of the most thoughtful of the Decembrists and leader of the southern party, wrote:

The events of 1812–15 showed so many overturned thrones, so many others set up, so many empires destroyed so many new ones founded, so many rulers banished and others recalled or recognized and banished again, so many revolutions carried through, so many changes effected, that all these events accustomed minds to revolutions, and the possibilities, and desirabilities of inciting them. Every age has its own distinguishing mark; the present is characterized by revolutionary ideas.

The transition from idealism to materialism was effected in part by pupils of the French Encyclopedists, later of the Positivists, Comte and Spencer, in part by Hegelians who gave an ironical turn to the idealism of their master and put it to the service of Marx's dialectical materialism. This latter current gained in momentum and was released in a rushing tide of revolutionary action by Lenin.

An important feature in the thought of the intelligentsia is their close connection with prevailing social conditions; they exhibited no great power in their grasp of purely abstract questions. Whatever excursions they might make in purely speculative realms, their base was sociological. The pamphleteers and other advocates of reform in the time of Catherine were concerned with the theory of the rights of man because these rights were so obviously being disregarded at home. Thus when the great empress discovered this practical turn in what she had apparently regarded merely as a game of words and ideas, she hastily abandoned her own literary indiscretions and turned her back on her friends. But the future lay not with the social dilettantism of Catherine, but with Novikov and the author of the *Journey from Petersburg to Moscow,* Radishev. Kirievskii wrote in the thirties, "Our philosophy must develop from our national life, must be created out of contemporary problems and the prevailing temper of our national and personal existence."

Apart from their historical importance, it must be admitted

that the Russian intellectuals of the nineteenth century were less original and creative and more imitative and adaptive than their Western counterparts. As emigrants many brought with them out of Russia little more than a spirit of rebellion and a sense of release from oppression; their minds were formed and their thought moulded by European masters. Their notions were peculiarly Russian only when they infused general philosophical ideas with Russian sentiment or applied their philosophy of history to Russian circumstances. Their attitude toward religion reflected variously the hostility of scientific materialism, the cold admissions of Western deism, the romanticism of Schelling's *Natur-philosophie* or the metaphysical precision of Hegel's idealism. Only the Slavophiles and more recently some of the philosophers of the emigration, like Berdyaev, attempted with any degree of success a fusion between the old Slavic-Byzantine tradition and modern Russian ideals and ideas.

Nevertheless Florovskii contends that the religious problem was the starting point of all the thought of the intelligentsia.

The significant decades [he writes], were a time not only of ideological controversies. They were also a decisive phase in the development of religious sentiment. "The majority of the Russian intelligentsia were undoubtedly religious (Sakulin)." Romanticism and "idealism" were exposed in all their ambiguity and equivocation. It was impossible to stand for long at the crossroads; the choice of a path was inevitable. To remain stationary was itself a choice. In the thirties in any case, even the "Westerners" were occupied with the religious and moral question no less than the future "Slavophiles." Even the socialist theory of the time was inextricably bound up with Christian ideology. There was a quest for a complete view of the universe; Bakunin is in this respect more characteristic than the others. It should be recalled that even the divisions among "Westerners" in the middle of the forties involved a religious subject, personal immortality. The religious character of

the "Western" program in its later phase is exposed with special
clarity in the well-known letter of Belinskii to Gogol (1847). Here
the whole controversy arises with special reference to a religious
program: "In your view the Russian people is the most religious
in the world. False! . . . Look more intently and you will be convinced that it is by nature a profoundly atheistic people. In it there
is still much superstition but no trace of real religion. Mystic exal-
tation is not in its nature. It has too much healthy rationality, clarity and mental poise for that and perhaps in this fact will lie the
magnitude of its future destiny." Here the atheistical prospect directly opposed the religious. Atheism is, however, itself an answer
to the religious question. Feuerbach's problem is no less a religious
one than Baader's. The philosophic enthusiasm of the thirties and
forties had a twofold result. For some it opened a way into the
Church, the way of religious revival, a religious apocatastasis of
thought and will. For others it was a way to skepticism and even
direct hostility to religion. This split or polarization of the Russian
elite occurred precisely on a religious plane.[3]

It is impossible here to deal with the systems of individual
representatives of the intelligentsia or to trace the influence of
the whole philosophic movement on theologians like Khomya-
kov, Solovev, Leontev, or in our own time Merezhkovskii,
Rozanov, Berdyaev and Bulgakov, on the so-called gnoseology
and on the members of the St. Petersburg *Religiozno-phi-
losophskaya Sobraniya,* the president of which was Sergii
Stragorodskii, Tikhon's and Peter's successor in the patriarchate.
In spite of their eclecticism Russian philosophical theology has
an intrinsic value and its history a fascination of its own. Its
influence outside its own limited sphere of academicians and
émigrés was singularly disproportionate to its output. Florovskii puts his finger on the difficulty in his phrase "the Russian elite." There was no way of implementing this kind of
thinking in popular thought and sentiment. The strictness of
the censorship, the power of the more conservative clergy, and

[3] *Op. cit.,* p. 246.

the activity of the High Procurator's agents offered too powerful opposition to the spread of even a spirit of inquiry and
reflection among the bulk of the faithful. The intellectuals
themselves were not above a certain snobbishness of mind.
Koshelev wrote of the "Lovers of Wisdom," a philosophical
discussion group which met at Odoyevskii's house, "Christian
doctrine seemed to us suitable only for the vulgar masses but
not for us."

The stimulus to Russian social thought came from without,
but the spirit of reform was a home product. The struggle for
the emancipation first of the serfs and then of Russian society
as a whole is the connecting link between speculations and
plans, thought and action. As Ivanov Razumnik remarks, the
final break between the intelligentsia and the imperial system
was the result of the reforms of 1861 when the cynicism of the
government's program of emancipation dawned. Upon the discovery that a century of agitation had rendered the serfs free
only to fill the pockets of the landlords, Slavophiles and Westerners, materialists and idealists, positivists and mystics united
in the passionate resolve that the rights of man should not only
be asserted but won, if necessary on the field of a civil war. As
early as 1853 Hertzen wrote in the bitterness of exile:

The emperor Nicholas can perform great works the true meaning of which escapes him. He can bend the sterile arrogance of
France and the haughty circumspection of England to his will. He
can call Constantinople Russian and Germany Muscovite. We have
not the least pity for these weaklings. What he cannot do is to prevent another league from forming behind his back. He cannot prevent Russian intervention from being the death blow to all the
monarchs of the continent, all reaction, and the beginning of an
armed, terrible and decisive social struggle. The imperial power of
the tsar will not survive this struggle. Victor or vanquished he belongs to the past; he is not Russian but profoundly German, German with a Byzantine veneer. He therefore doubly deserves death.

But we have a double claim to life: The socialist element and youth.

The phrase "socialist element" is significant. The notion that the old order must go and a new emancipated order take its place grew in strength and became a moral conviction transcending particular parties and groups. Upon this moral conviction was constructed the coming Russian doctrine of man.

Chapter III

ANTIRELIGIOUS THEORY IN RUSSIA

IN ESTIMATING THE THOUGHT LYING BEHIND revolutionary aims and action in Russia it is well to note that the leaders of the discontented masses were themselves highly discontented men. Marx's radical temper and aggressive literary manner as much as his ideas roused an instinctive opposition among the conservative and more comfortably placed and he became an exile wandering from Germany to England, France and Belgium in search of freedom to compose and publish his works. Engels' early quarrels with his family and clashes with the business interests which they represented made him the social and political *enfant terrible* of the Rhineland. Lenin was embittered by his brother's arrest and exile and became the champion of the cause of which his brother was an accredited martyr. Plekhanov fell an early victim of political persecution and fled to France. Stalin had been expelled from the theological seminary at Tiflis for liberal views and later consigned to Siberia as an agitator. Most of the leaders of the early stage of the Revolution had suffered for their convictions, many had political prison records and all felt as vengeful against the old order as they were confident in the new. Their lives were microcosms of the social upheavals they initiated, setting the tone of aggressive discontent and turning the tide of violent insurgence.

For the position of religion in the new order two aspects of

Communist philosophy are important: its view of the nature and social function of religion, and its theory of social evolution.

The origins of all Russian revolutionary thought are to be found in the works of Karl Marx and Friedrich Engels. Marx became preoccupied with religion as a philosophical matter in his student days. From Hegel he learned to regard philosophy as an alternative to theology and from Kant and Schelling, in his Munich period, he mastered the current philosophic criticism of religious tradition. It is characteristic that he selected for his doctor's dissertation a treatment of two Greek materialists, Democritus and Epicurus. In the *Vorarbeiten,* notebooks written before 1841, the following illuminating passage occurs:

The proofs for the existence of God are nothing but empty tautologies, e.g., the ontological proof amounts to no more than saying, "What I actually (really) conceive is an actual conception for me," which influences me and in this sense all gods, pagan and Christian have real existence. Did not Moloch have his own sphere of influence? Was not the Delphic Oracle an actual force in the life of the Greeks? . . . Bring paper money into a country where this use of paper is unknown, and everyone will laugh at your subjective notion. Go with your gods to a land where other gods are worshipped and it will be proven to you that you suffer from fancies and errors. Rightly. If any one had brought a god of the Wends to Greece, he would have been met with a proof of the nonexistence of this god, for to the Greeks he did not exist. What a particular country means for gods foreign to that country, is the area of reason for God in general. It is a territory in which his existence ceases.

Or the proofs for the existence of God are nothing but proofs for the existence of actual human self-consciousness and its logical explanations, e.g., the ontological proof. What being is directly given by thinking of it? Consciousness of self. In this sense all proofs for the existence of God are proofs of his nonexistence. The actual proof must run contrariwise, "Because nature is badly constructed, there is a God. Because the universe is irrational, there is a God. Because thought does not exist, there is a God." What confirms this, however, when, "God exists for him to whom the world is irrational, who therefore is himself irrational? In other words, the existence of God is irrationality."

In these jottings, especially in the concluding Feuerbachian observations Marx's later views on the nature of religion are anticipated. Philosophically religion depends upon metaphysical confusion; experientially it may lead man to a fuller knowledge of himself but never to a clearer view of the universe. As an Hegelian of the old school Marx bitterly resented Schelling's appearance in Berlin as Hegel's critic and his attempt to re-evaluate religious tradition. In an earlier passage of the *Vorarbeiten* he quotes from Schelling's *Letters on Dogmatism,* "Reason is not weak when it fails to recognize God but when it wishes to do so," and "It is high time to proclaim freedom of the spirit to the better part of mankind and no longer to tolerate its weeping over the loss of its chains," and comments ironically, "If it was time to do this in 1795 how about 1841?"

In accepting the necessity for modifying Hegel's views Marx attached himself to the Hegelian Left Wing and with characteristic fury hurled himself into violent polemic against all who interpreted his master differently from himself. In a pamphlet written against Schelling in 1843 he explains that Hegel's influence became widespread only after his death when both its power and its limitations became apparent. These limitations, in Marx's view, were most evident in Hegel's theological opinions. He writes:

[Hegel's] philosophy of religion and law would have certainly turned out quite differently if he had abstracted more of those positive elements which he had acquired from the education of his day, and had developed these themes from pure thought. All inconsistencies and contradictions in Hegel can be reduced to this error. Everything that appears too orthodox in the philosophy of religion and too pseudo-historical in his political theory is to be explained from this point of view. The principles are always independent and spontaneous, the consequences, no one will deny, are occasionally restricted, even illiberal. For this reason a group of his pupils arose who retained the principles and rejected the consequences when they could not be justified. The Left Wing formed, Ruge gave it a means of expression in the *Hallischen Jahrbüchern* and one night the break with the positive elements was made. Still no one ventured to bring all the consequences of this into the open. Even after Strauss it was believed that Hegelianism was essentially Christian and boasts were made to the Jews of its Christian character. There was not enough clarity on such questions as the personality of God and individual immortality to permit decisive judgments to be formed. There was even some doubt when the inevitable consequences dawned, whether the new teaching should not remain the private property of the [Hegelian] school and kept a secret from the nation. [The work of the Hegelian left made it abundantly clear that] all the fundamental premises of Christianity, indeed of what man had in general considered religion to be, had fallen before the merciless criticism of reason. The absolute Idea claimed to be the founder of a new era. The great revolution, of which the French philosophers of the previous century had only been the precursors, achieved completion in the realm of thought. . . . The philosophy of Protestantism, from Descartes on was finished. A new period has opened and it is the most sacred duty of all who have followed the self-development of Spirit to transpose the tremendous result into the consciousness of the nation and to raise it to a life principle of Germany.

The new Hegelianism stripped of theological encumbrances was nothing else than the new materialism which had its antecedents in French thought of the end of the eighteenth century. The last sentence, however, hints at its novel historical application, Marx's dialectical materialism with its own peculiar interpretation of the nature of society and the historical process.

The militant note presages the reforming, revolutionary spirit of Marxian thought.

It is unnecessary for us here to consider the development of the purely philosophic aspects of Marxian materialism. For his theory of religion, his view of the interrelation of religious and economic factors in the social organism is of primary importance. This question is first raised and Marx's basic principles defined in an early essay on the Jewish question in a review of Bruno Bauer's work on that subject. Bauer suggested that the emancipation of the Jews could be accomplished, if Jews and Christians both abandoned their divisive religious attachments and met on the common ground of rationalism. Marx objected to this religious solution of the problem on the ground that the roots of the difficulty lay not in religious principles but in social attitudes.

We shall attempt [he writes] to break with the theological consideration of the problem. The question of the capacity of the Jews for emancipation merges for us into the question, what particular social element must be overcome in order to eliminate Judaism? For the capacity for emancipation among contemporary Jews is the relation of Judaism to the emancipation of the contemporary world. The relation is determined by the peculiar position of Judaism in the contemporary enslaved world.

Let us consider the actual secular Jew, not the Sabbath-Jew, as Bauer does, but the everyday Jew. Let us look for the Jew's secret not in his religion but let us look for the secret of religion in the actual Jew. What is the secular law of Judaism? Practical need, self-interest. What is the secular culture of the Jew? The usurer. What is his secular god? Money. Therefore the emancipation from the usurer and from money, i.e., from practical, real Judaism would be the self-emancipation of our time. . . . We recognize therefore in Judaism a general contemporary, anti-social element which has reached its present height through the historical development with which the Jews have in this evil respect zealously co-operated. At this level it must be dissolved. The emancipation of the Jew is in

the last analysis, the emancipation of humanity from Judaism. . . .
Because the real nature of the Jew has realized and secularized itself in bourgeois society, this society cannot convince the Jew of
the unreality of his religious nature, for the latter is only an ideal
view of practical need. We find, therefore, the nature of the contemporary Jew not only in the Pentateuch or in the Talmud but in
contemporary society where he functions not as an abstract but as
a highly empirical being. The problem is not so much the limitation of the Jew as the Jewish limitation of society. . . . The social
emancipation of the Jew is the emancipation of society from
Judaism.

It is possible to read between the lines of this account indica-
tions of Marx's growing conviction that religion was engendered not only by individual needs, as Feuerbach had maintained,
but by social situations of which it was a kind of symptom
or property. The important feature of contemporary Judaism
in Marx's view was not its religious ideals but its behavior
pattern and the plain implications of that pattern. The Jew
might worship in a synagogue but he did his business in a
bank, and it was in this way his social influence was felt.
Furthermore, the economic conditions which made banking
profitable and a source of power evoked this Jewish behavior
pattern and supplied it with its real motivation. The Jews did
not produce the spirit of the age but epitomize and incorporate
it. This spirit does not distinguish Jews from Christians absolutely, but relatively. It infuses the lives of both but to an
unequal degree.

The clearest, fullest expression of Marx's theory of religion is
found in the well-known passage at the beginning of his
Critique of Hegel's Philosophy of Law written in 1843. It reads:

For Germany the criticism of religion is essentially finished and
the criticism of religion is the premise of all criticism. The secular
existence of error is compromised once its heavenly *oratio pro aris
et focis* has been refuted. Man who sought a superman in the fan-

tasy reality of heaven, has only discovered a reflexion of himself and will no more be inclined to find only the reflexion of himself, only an inhuman being, where he seeks and must seek reality.

The foundation of irreligious criticism is that "man makes religion, not religion makes man." Religion is man's consciousness and awareness of himself when he has either not come into his own or has lost himself. Man is, however, no abstract being crouching outside the world. Man is man's world and includes state and society. State and society produce religion which is a perverse apprehension of the world because they comprise a perverse world. Religion is this world's general view, its compendium of fact, its logic in popular form, its spiritual enthusiasm, its moral sanction, its devotional complement, its general ground of consolation and justification. It is the realization in fantasy of human nature, because human nature possesses no true reality. The struggle against religion is therefore immediately the struggle against that world the spiritual aroma of which religion is.

Religious misery is both the expression of real misery and a protest against real misery. Religion is the sigh of the oppressed creature, the temper of a heartless world, as it is the spirit of inanimate circumstances. *It is the people's opium.*

The abolition of religion as the people's illusory happiness is a requisite of their real happiness. The requirement to abandon illusions about their condition is the requirement to give up a state of things which requires illusions. The criticism of religion is therefore in nucleus the criticism of the vale of misery the sanctified reflection of which religion is.

The influence of Feuerbach is again obvious in the theory that religion has only subjective validity. It offers a means for self-discovery, not for a discovery of God. Marx's own thought, however, is to be seen in his dismissal of the notion that man exists as an individual at all. "Man is man's world and includes state and society."

In a notebook he wrote in criticism of Feuerbach:

Feuerbach dissolves the religious being into the human being. But the human being is not an abstraction immanent in the individual being. In actuality he is an ensemble of social relationships. . . . Feuerbach does not see that the religious sentiment itself is a social product and that the abstract individual which he analyzes belongs to a particular social form . . . the standpoint of the old materialism is middle class society; the standpoint of the new is human society or social humanity.

Religion thus reflects social conditions and because the latter are confused and perverse, religion is also confused and perverse and permits no clear vision of objective truth.

It is important to pause for a moment on the much abused phrase, Religion is the people's opium, for its meaning derives from its context. Later critics often use the phrase as if it meant that the religious drug had been administered by the exploiting classes to an unwary proletariat, but this is not the sense of the passage. Religion is a pipe dream to exploited and exploiter alike. Its materials are those of common experience but the proportions, perspectives, and values of actuality are distorted. The drug consists of those unwholesome elements in the social ferment which compel him to seek consolation and emotional color in illusion. Its aroma arises from conditions as they are and the only remedy is to change the conditions and eliminate the drug.

This emphasis on action is important, for it points the way to the Marxian doctrine of revolution. In the private notes on Feuerbach he observes:

The principal lack of materialism thus far (including Feuerbach's) is that the object, reality, sensual perception is regarded only under the form of the object or view, not as human activity and practice involving the senses; not subjectively. Feuerbach wants sensually perceived objects actually distinct from the objects of thought but he does not conceive human activity itself as objective activity. In the *Essence of Christianity,* therefore, he observes only the theoretical attitude as genuinely human while practice is conceived and secured only in its filthy Jewish form of appearance. He does not understand, therefore, the significance of the "revolutionary," "practical-united" activity. . . . All social life is essentially a matter of practice. All mysteries which occasion mystical theories, find their rational solution in human practice and in the understanding of that practice. . . . The philosophers have only interpreted the world in various ways; the important thing is to change it.

In a later passage of his review of Hegel's *Philosophy of Law* he says:

Criticism has plucked the imaginary flowers from the chain, not in order that man should wear a chain bereft of fancy and consolation but that he may cast off the chain and pick real flowers. The criticism of religion disillusions man in order that he may think, act and mould reality like a disillusioned man who has come to his senses, in order that he may do something about himself and about his real sun. Religion is only the illusory sun, which moves about man only as long as man does not act for himself.

The remedy for the opiate, then, is vigorous action in the world of reality in order to improve man's lot. Marx envisages his liberated human being as rousing himself from his couch, shaking off the effects of his long, dream-laden sleep and going about his business in the light of common day.

It is no doubt only a step from this conclusion to the view that religion is an instrument of class exploitation, but Marx's main thesis was that religion had been an inevitable, evil accompaniment of an inevitable, evil process. Its qualities derived from the social evolution of which it was the product and this evolution was determined by fixed and immutable laws. Religion might furnish the terms on which the masses were exploited but the ultimate facts, as Marx had pointed out in his essay on the Jewish question, were economic and social. Change the substance of the social situation and such accidents as religion would yield automatically. Let the proletariat arise and victoriously transform the social order, as is enjoined in the Communist Manifesto. Then the haunting dream of religion would be forgotten in the excitement and bustle of the new revolutionary era.

In the Hegelian system the absolute Idea realized itself in the process of history. The Hegelian Left substituted matter and motion in evolution for the Idea, but the importance of the historical ramifications of the earlier Hegelianism gained rather than lost by this transformation. The originality of Marx and Engels lay in their claim that economic forces were the primary conditioning factors in history. This theory was applied to the growth of society in general in the Communist Manifesto (1848), written jointly by Marx and Engels. Its relevance for the history of religion was seen by Marx but applied by Engels and after him, by the Russian Marxists. In this they depended much on the materials collected by the rationalist historians of religion in France and England and on the method of Feuerbach.

The influence of Feuerbach on antireligious criticism was paradoxical, for Feuerbach himself felt that his explanation of religion as a purely subjective experience aided in its appreciation and was indeed the only way of restoring its credit among educated men. This apologetic attitude was antipathetic to Marx and Engels and even more to the Russian Marxists, who therefore turned for support in their antireligious campaign to the Encyclopedists and their followers. In his essay on *Socialism and Religion,* Lenin wrote:

Our program is built on science and in particular on the materialistic view of the world. The clarification of our program includes necessarily therefore the clarification of the true historical and economic grounds of the religious fog. Our propaganda necessarily includes also atheistic propaganda: Editions of appropriate scientific literature which the imperial government has hitherto strictly prohibited and forbidden, should now form one of the branches of our party work. We should probably now act on the advice Engels once gave the German Socialists for the translation in mass of the French rationalist and atheistic literature of the nineteenth century.

In writing of his own contribution to the Marxian system, Engels wrote:

I cannot deny that both before and during my forty years of collaboration with Marx I had a certain independent share in laying the foundations and more particularly in elaborating the theory. But the greater part of its leading basic principles, particularly in the realm of economics and history, and above all its final, clear, formulation, belong to Marx.

Part of Engel's share in "elaborating the theory" was his treatment of religion. Religion, in Engel's view, arose as a corollary to the theory of immortality suggested to savages by dreams of dead persons.

Not religious desire for consolation, but the quandary arising from the common universal ignorance of what to do with the soul (once its existence had been accepted) after the death of the body and led in a general way to the tedious notion of personal immortality. In an exactly similar manner the first gods arose through the personification of natural forces. And these gods in the further development of religion assumed more and more an extra-mundane force, until finally by the process of abstraction, I might almost say of distillation, occurring naturally in the course of man's intellectual development, out of many more or less limited and mutually limiting gods there arose in the minds of men the idea of the one exclusive god of the non-atheistic religions.

Monotheism raised the question of creation and by implication the whole question of the relation of the world of thought to the material order of nature. Philosophers divided on the question of the primacy of thought over matter and the result was the conflict of idealism versus materialism. The weakness of eighteenth century materialism was that it tended to be static. It saw the world rightly in terms of mechanics but failed to see it as a process. It was not until the nineteenth century that the idea of evolution pervaded the natural sciences and revealed nature in its dynamic aspects, as moving not in a circle but forward according to a fixed pattern. From natural science this notion was transposed to the historical and social sciences which revealed their own types of evolution.

In one point [writes Engels] the history of the development of society proves to be essentially different from that of nature. In nature—in so far as we ignore man's reactions upon nature—there are only blind unconscious agencies acting upon one another and out of whose interplay the general laws come into operation. Nothing of all that happens—whether in the innumerable apparent accidents observable upon the surface of things, or in the ultimate results which confirm the regularity underlying these accidents— is attained as a consciously desired aim. In the history of society, on the other hand, the actors are all endowed with consciousness, are men acting with deliberation or passion, working towards definite goals; nothing happens without a conscious purpose, without an intended aim. But this distinction, important as it is for historical investigation, particularly of single epochs and events, cannot alter the fact that the course of hstory is governed by inner general laws. For here, also, on the whole, in spite of the consciously desired aims of all individuals, accident apparently reigns on the surface. That which is willed happens but rarely; in the majority of instances the numerous desired ends cross and conflict with one another, or these ends themselves are from the outset incapable of realisation or the means of attaining them are insufficient. Thus the conflict of innumerable individual wills and individual actions in the domain of history produces a state of affairs entirely analogous to that in the realm of unconscious nature. The

ends of the actions are intended, but the results which actually
follow from these actions are not intended; or when they do seem
to correspond to the end intended, they ultimately have consequences quite other than those intended. Historical events thus
appear on the whole to be likewise governed by chance. But where
on the surface accident holds sway, there actually it is always governed by inner, hidden laws and it is only a matter of discovering
these laws.

Differentiation in the evolution of society is created by economic causes which result in the stratification, dislocation, and
ultimately the liberation of class society. The evolution of political and social thought both reflects and interacts with that of
political and social life. "The state presents itself to us as the
first ideological power over mankind." Other ideologies, however, arise. Law, philosophy, and even religion emerge in the
ever complicating process of social evolution. In the latter,
however, "the inter-connection between the ideas and their
material conditions of existence becomes more and more complicated, and more and more obscured by intermediate links."
Religion arose from primitive and mistaken notions about man
and his natural environment which, however, reflected the
structure of the social life in which he was engaged. With the
rise of nationalities, national gods appeared which maintained
themselves in connection with the political entities which gave
them birth and tended to disappear with their decline. When
the Roman Empire created a supranational state there was a
demand for a new and more comprehensive religion and
Christianity arose, molding such a faith from the materials of
Judaism and popular paganism. The Roman Empire merged
into its successors the Christian empires of the East and West.

The rise of the *bourgeoisie* coincided with the beginnings of
town life and commercialism in the Middle Ages. The order
of the economic day was not unity but difference, not control

but competition. Protestantism and the sects registered this change:

To the masses whose minds were fed with religion to the exclusion of all else, it was necessary to put forward their own interests in a religious guise in order to produce a great agitation. And since the *bourgeoisie* from the beginning brought into being an appendage of propertyless urban plebeians, day-labourers and servants of all kinds, belonging to no recognized social estate, precursors of the later proletariat, so likewise heresy soon became divided into a bourgeois moderate heresy and a plebeian revolutionary one, the latter an abomination to the bourgeois heretics themselves.[1]

Lutheranism proved an inadequate vehicle of the *bourgeoisie* but Calvinism "justified itself as the true religious disguise of the interests" of that class. This disguise was shed in France in the eighteenth century by the rationalists and revolutionaries. "Instead of Protestants, free-thinkers took their place in the national assemblies. Thereby Christianity entered on its final stage." It had become incapable for the future of serving any progressive class as the ideological garb of its aspirations.

It is obvious that the importance of that theory is not to be sought in the soundness of its historical judgment. Its analysis of neither the origins of religion in general, nor of the history of Christianity in particular is impressive. It served, however, as a paradigm of later more developed Marxian views. The pattern of interaction between economic class interests and the ideologies which they engendered could be and was variously drawn and with varying degrees of historical competence and acumen.

It is time to turn our attention to the history of Russian Marxism and to trace the development of thought about religion

[1] Extracts from Engel's *Ludwig Feuerbach* have been made from the English translation in the Marxist Library, vol. xv (New York: International Publishers Co., Inc., 1935).

and its role in society among the precursors of Lenin and Stalin. The influence of Marx and Engels on Russian thought came by way of the intelligentsia and for some forty years remained sporadic and incidental. Through Ruge, Marx made the acquaintance of Bakunin in Paris; a lively exchange of views and letters followed. In spite of some common sympathies, however, there was a lack of personal rapport between the two men and a sharp divergence on their views on Russia. Years later Bakunin wrote: "[Marx] called me a sentimental idealist and was right; I called him a sinister, disloyal and vain man and was equally right."

In Russia, as elsewhere, Marx's views were accepted in some circles with reservations. Shifts in emphasis and changes in the corollaries to the main principles were advocated. For Lenin, however, the Marxian system was not a theory but a dogma. It was bred by the revolutionary spirit and was the only adequate reflection of its aims and program. It was not subject to revision and attempts to modify it were heresy and indicated an imperfect apprehension of the meaning of revolution. In his only purely philosophical work, the essay *Materialism and Empiro-criticism,* Lenin attacked the revisionists of the reactionary period with the same bitter ferocity with which Marx had opposed Bauer and Stirner, on the ground that they had given away the essence of their case. Their criticism of Marx and Engels are concessions not only to a theoretically indefensible, but to a practically obstructionst, idealism. They represent, he says, "a typical philosophical revisionism, for only revisionists acquire pathetic distinction by their retreat from the fundamental views of Marxism and by their fear or incapacity openly, directly, decisively and clearly to settle their accounts with the opinions they have abandoned." It is necessary to trace the real drift of these concessions, to trace their source in a new German philosophy, the empiro-criticism of Ernst Mach and Avenarius which conceals its covert readmission of idealism under misleading phrases. Above all it is essential to see the social implications of revisionism. In the conclusion of his essay he writes:

In the gnoseological scholasticism of empiro-criticism it is impossible not to see a party struggle in philosophy, a struggle which in the last analysis reflects the tendencies and ideology of the opposing classes in contemporary society. The latest philosophy is as much a party creed as it was two thousand years ago. However much the fact may be concealed by novel clichés and witless claims to nonpartisanship, the parties in conflict are essentially materialism and idealism. The latter is only a subtle and refined form of fideism which stands well-armed, with powerful organizations at its disposal and steadily continues its influence on the masses, appropriating to its use the slightest turn in the direction of philosophic thought. The actual role of empiro-criticism in the class struggle in every way favors conciliation with the fideists in their struggle against materialism in general and historical materialism in particular.

It is evident that for Lenin any deviation from classical Marxianism must serve as a cloak for social passivity and a return to religion as the principal guarantee of that passivity.

At no point is Lenin more completely at one with the ideas and temper of Marx than in his attitude toward religion. As in his revolutionary thinking he is more Marxian than Marx, so in his critique of religion he is a more violent and aggressive enemy of faith. In a letter written to Gorkii in 1913 he speaks his mind with characteristically uninhibited vigor:

The difference between seeking God and constructing or creating or inventing etc., a God is no greater than between a yellow or a blue devil. It is a hundred times worse than saying nothing to speak of a search for God, unless one intends to attack all devils and gods, all spiritual necrophilia. Every divinity involves necrophilia; it makes no difference how pure and ideal or how created, not sought, he may be. The more refined and critical theology becomes, the more socially enticing and dangerous it becomes. [Such liberal theology is] the most dangerous vulgarity, the foulest infection, because every religious idea, any idea of any god, any flirtation with (the idea of) a god is an unspeakable vulgarity willingly tolerated and often enthusiastically accepted by the democratic *bourgeoisie*. A million sins, bestialities, rapes, and infections of a physical kind are more easily seen through by the crowd and therefore less dangerous than the refined spiritualized idea of God decked out in the most gorgeous costume.

The social preoccupations lying behind this estimate of religion is as apparent as in Marx's lucubrations on the same theme. It is explicit in Lenin's statement from a latter portion of the letter to Gorkii:

From the social, from the personal standpoint, every theory of God is nothing but the adoring self-concern of the stupid *petite bourgeoisie,* of the destructive middle class spirit.

Lenin's formal treatment of the religious question is found in three essays: *Socialism and Religion, On the Relation of the Workers' Party to Religion,* and *Classes and Parties in Their Relation to Religion and the Church.* The first of these was published in 1905 in the December number of the Communist organ *Novaya Zhizn,* the editorship of which Lenin had assumed the preceding month. It contains a general statement of his views and should be read in the larger context of his campaign at this time to reorganize the Workers' party, clarify their program and enable them to present a united front. He reiterates the Marxian thesis that contemporary society is based "on the exploitation of the huge masses of the working class by an insignificant minority belonging to the classes of land-owners and capitalists," and claims that the social function of religion is to obscure this picture and befuddle the workers with visions of imaginary satisfactions to compensate for real privations. He pleads for the program which he was later to put into effect, the complete separation of the Church from the state and education from the Church:

The state should have no concern for religion [he writes], and religious societies should not be connected with the government. Everyone should be completely free to profess any religion he chooses, or to accept no religion at all, i.e., to be an atheist as every socialist usually is. The Russian revolution should realize this demand as an essential and integral part of political freedom.

He protests, however, against the view accepted as a compromise by the German Social Democrats since 1875 and incorporated in the Erfurt Program of 1891 that religion was a private matter and should be left out of the party program.

In relation to the party of the socialist proletariat, religion is not a private matter. Our party is a union of conscious, progressive contestants for the liberation of the working class. Such a union can and must not be indifferent to unawareness, obscurantism and obfuscation in the form of religious convictions. We demand complete separation of the Church from the state in order to combat the religious fog with purely intellectual and only intellectual weapons, our press and our words. We have, however, founded our union, the Revolutionary Social Democratic Party of Workers, among other things, especially for such a struggle against the religious deception of the workers. For us the intellectual conflict is not a private affair but a matter of concern for the whole party, the whole proletariat.

The essay *Materialism and Empiro-criticism* appeared in May, 1905. The later essays on religion were written almost simultaneously in May and June of the same year and issue from the same stratum of thought. The first *On the relation of the Workers' Party to Religion* served as an editorial comment to an attack on religion made by the Bolshevik deputy Surkov on April 27, 1909 at the third Duma. Here Lenin restates his disagreement with the Erfurt decision that religion was a private matter, declaring that "Social Democracy considers religion a private matter in relation to the state but never in relation to itself or to Marxism or to the Workers' Party." Marxism is a materialist philosophy and as such is hostile to religion but Marx stressed the dynamic, functional importance of thought and Lenin insists that the characteristic feature of Marxian socialism is its call to action. Marx, he says, goes further than the theoretical materialists when he claims that "it is necessary to fight religion and therefore necessary to explain the origins of faith and religion among the masses in materialistic terms." The bourgeois progressive, the radical or bourgeois materialist seeks the roots of religion in popular ignorance and its cure in antireligious propaganda and the spread of atheistic opinion. The roots of religion, however, are not intellectual but social and the masses must be brought to see the connection between the prevalence of religion and the dominance of capital. This blind force which has overwhelmed the workers who serve it is the real root of religion. In backing the one, the proletariat must exterminate the other.

This dynamic activist conception of religion leads Lenin to formulate his own peculiar notion of religious toleration. Religion in each of its phases must be judged by its immediate contemporary effect on society. It is conceivable that in some social and historical situations a provisional toleration of religion or at best of religiously minded persons may serve the ultimate cause of the liberation of the masses better than militant opposition.

For example [he writes], the question often arises, "Can a priest become a member of the Social-Democratic Party?" This question is usually answered without any reservations, arguing from the experience of the European Social-Democratic Parties. But this experience has arisen not only from the application of the Marxists doctrine to the Labor Movement but also under the peculiar circumstances of the West which do not obtain in Russia.

The correct view is that a priest who is prepared *ex animo* and without reserve to serve the party should be admitted to it. If, on the other hand, he should use his position in the party to spread his religious views which run counter to the party's official ideology, he should be excluded.

A more immediate question is that raised by Lunacharskii's thesis that socialism was a personal religion in its own right. Lenin here warns against being taken in by words. Such a theory, he admits, is irreconcilable with Marxism or even with Socialism but its advocacy must be judged in its immediate social and historical context. If it is advanced by a convinced socialist as the official view of the party, it will retard the development of the masses. If, however, it be expressed by a partial convert to socialism as an advance over a previously held, more conservative opinion, it should be encouraged as a step in the right direction. Lenin concludes: "For some the thesis, socialism is a religion, is a form of transition from religion to socialism; for others from socialism to religion."

Lenin's third essay, *Classes and Parties in Their Relation to Religion and the Church,* is also in the nature of an editorial comment on debates in the Duma on the Synod, the restoration of rights to persons with clerical vocations, and on the position of the Old Believers. Here Lenin warns against the revival of a militant clericalism represented in the Duma by what he describes as "not only bureaucrats in cassocks as Surkov has called them, but landlords in cassocks," whose power had been consistently underestimated by the Nationalists and Liberals. This revival Lenin interprets as an attempt on the part of the *bourgeoisie* to recapture its control over the workers. In contrast with the feeble qualifications of the liberals he quotes Surkov's words, "not a penny of the people's money . . . should go to these bloody enemies of the people who darken the popular consciousness," and comments, "This direct, courageous, open and hostile cry of a socialist sounded like a summons to the Black Hundred Duma and resounded in the hearts of millions of the proletariat who will spread it among the masses who can, when the time comes, translate it into revolutionary action."

In spite of their differences of opinion on the political evolution of Russia and on the means to effect reform, the relations between Lenin and Plekhanov in the criticism of religion were similar to those of Marx and Engels. Lenin enunciated the broad principles and pointed out their relevance to the larger issues of social changes; Plekhanov concerned himself more in detail with the professional literature on the nature and history of religion. Notes of a lecture on Scientific Socialism and Religion, given at a socialist congress in Zurich in 1904, have been recently published along with reprints of his reviews of various works on religious and philosophical subjects and his own extensive treatise, *On the So-called Religious Quests in Russia*. With the exception of the first lecture, these compositions came from the period of reaction after the revolt of 1905 and are parallel to Lenin's works of the same period. They are directed against the current liberal movements in theology called *Bogoiskatelstvo* and *Bogostroitelstvo* which were viewed with suspicion both by the official Orthodoxy and official Communism but which each was willing to encourage as weapons against the other. Neither was, however, inclined to permit free access or much alleged currency to the views of such men as Merezhkovskii, Hippius and Philosov or of Berdyaev and Bulgakov.

The work on religious quests opens with a discussion of the nature of religion in the usual Feuerbachian style. It marks an advance, however, in incorporating the more recent anthropological and historical work of English, French, and German scholars. It passes quickly to a critical review of contemporary tendencies in Russian religious thought, deals with Tolstoy, Lunacharskii, Gorkii as author of the *Confession,* and ends with a biting chapter on the "Gospel of Decadence," as he describes the theories of Merezhkovskii and Minskii.

The importance of Plekhanov as a critic of religion lies not in the originality of his views but in his ability to provide the current Marxian formulae with substance and learning. In contrast with Lenin he is a man of thought rather than of action. His works had contemporary propagandistic value but the road from Marx to the Moscow of 1917 leads through Lenin's essays of 1905 and 1909 and by-passes Plekhanov. The break between Lenin and Plekhanov on party issues and the alliance of the latter with the Mensheviks discredited him too much to permit his influence on early revolutionary thought to be great. A reprint of his works on antireligious writings appeared under the auspices of the Russian State Public Library in 1939.

Until World War II, Stalin followed Lenin in supporting a militant antireligious campaign, although he appears to have been less preoccupied with this question than Lenin and some of the other early leaders. His present attitude is an enigma. As late as 1936, however, he wrote in his essay *Marxism and the Colonial Question*:

Social Democracy will always protest against the persecution of Catholicism and Protestantism. We shall always defend the right of a nation to profess any religion it pleases. But at the same time, we shall take our departure from the rightly understood interests of the proletariat, and will agitate against Catholicism and Protestantism and even Orthodoxy in order to assure victory to the socialist view of the world.

At the outbreak of the Revolution of 1917, Lenin and his friends found themselves in a position to put their theories into practice and were prepared. Ideology had to be translated into propaganda, stated in simple terms and put across with emo-

tional conviction. Marx had declared the need to fight religion
and Lenin had enthusiastically concurred. This war now began. Its battalions were the godless societies and atheistic groups
in the Komsomol.

The materials and technique of atheistic propaganda will be
considered later. Here it should be noted that whereas the
atheism of Communist propaganda was more vehement in tone
than in theoretical discussions, its content suffered. Ideas were
more loosely and less cogently presented; arguments were
valued by their immediate appeal to popular feeling. Characteristic of this phase is the work of Yaroslavskii, for many years
president of the League of Militant Atheists and the most
active promoter of the campaign against religion in Russia.
In a book *Religion in the U.S.S.R.,* written for foreign con-
sumption, he offers an excellent example of the temper, not of
well considered philosophical, but of popular antireligious
thought.

The conception of the world from the religious point of view
[he writes], is incorrect; . . . it is a mutilated understanding of
the world and of the mutual relationships of men. A person cannot
act correctly, cannot act in an organized manner as a Communist,
as a Leninist if his brain is poisoned by religion. . . . Religion acts
as a bandage over the eyes of man, preventing him from seeing the
world as it is.

As with the philosophers of the Revolution, the propagandists
are primarily concerned with action, not ideas.

If the world is controlled by God [naïvely writes Yaroslavskii],
if the fate of the people is in the hands of God, his saints, angels,
devils and fiends—then what sense is there in the organized struggle of the workers and peasants, in the creation of a Leninist party?
What sense is there in the socialist reconstruction of society? All
this could be destroyed by a mere wave of the "Almighty Hand of

God"—who, happily, exists only in the imagination of believers—nowhere else!

The total impression produced by Communist philosophy, especially in its attitude to religion, is somewhat bewildering. The world which has been created on its principle is unprecedented and startlingly new. A utopia of human achievement has risen before the incredulous eyes of Western Europe and America defying all predictions and outraging many economic prejudices and social sensibilities. Now that this world has come into being, however, the ideas which first sustained its builders seem almost grotesquely old-fashioned and unrelated to contemporary thought. Lenin's suggestion for translations en masse of the atheistic literature of the eighteenth century has been quite literally followed and cheap editions of works no longer read outside of Russia, except by historians, circulate as current reading. Contemporary Russian studies of religion are little more than the reworking of familiar themes and are thin and poor in quality and quantity. Russian philosophic studies on materialism are hardly better and follow a depressingly uniform mode. All doubts are resolved by quotations from the Communist canon of Scripture, the works of Marx, Engels, Lenin, and Stalin. These are in a class by themselves and are invariably cited with fervor.

There appears no understanding and no will to understand the universe in any other but a strictly dogmatic way. The conquest of nature has opened unlimited horizons, but the realm of thought contains for the orthodox Bolshevik no new and open vistas. Even in natural science, the Russians who, in time of war, have continued to think hard and well, have been most productive in novel applications rather than novel principles.

The explanation of this anomaly is to be found in this role which thought has played in Russian revolutionary life. This role has always been secondary. Programs, schemes, plans for achieving practical results have been primary. Marx viewed his own thinking as means to an end and this has been even more conspicuously true of his Russian followers.

It is not surprising therefore that as the program was assured of realization, intellectual curiosity, moral unrest, and spiritual hunger should reassert themselves and it is highly significant that this tendency has resulted in a return to the past, not an attempt to pick up the dropped threads of contact with liberal European thought. The revival of Orthodoxy since the war, is in part an intellectual renaissance, evoked by the narrowness and inadequacy of the earlier revolutionary philosophy. This return may appear on the surface regressive and defeatist, but it is due fundamentally to the insistence of facts neglected and excluded by the materialists, the facts of spiritual life. Because these facts are very simple, but very puzzling, it has always been easier for sophisticated minds to rule them out of court, but they refuse to be snubbed, bide their time and take revenge ultimately by suddenly redominating the scene.

It must be admitted that neither the persistence of the old materialism, nor the revival of Orthodoxy gives immediate promise of new and vigorous intellectual developments. The importance of the government's recent concessions to the Church is that they constitute the first encouragement given since 1917 to a rival ideology. It is a hopeful precedent, the effect of which must inevitably be to broaden sympathies, widen prevailing views and take the sting out of Soviet dogmatism. In a country which for twenty-five years has released so much constructive energy, liberated so many from harsh political, economic, and cultural disabilities, it is inconceivable that intellectual power will not demand its own freedoms and insist on its own autonomy. The gentle cynic may take quiet amusement, but also heart in the fact that the first official gesture toward religion by the Soviet government of a liberal and tolerant kind, recognizes and ratifies the assertion of the ancient faith.

Chapter IV

THE ATTACK ON RELIGIOUS
INSTITUTIONS

O N THE TWENTY-FIFTH OF OCTOBER, THE
Bolshevik Revolution began in Petrograd and spread rapidly
to other cities and towns and ultimately engulfed the whole
country. Its effect upon all classes of society was immediate
and drastic. The impact of the movement upon the Church was
peculiarly dramatic since it came in the midst of the long hoped
for reforming council and overshadowed the day of the restoration of the patriarchate. Next to the imperial government
itself, the Church was an immediate objective of Communist
attack. It was a state Church and embodied in its social teaching
and influence all the tendencies most characteristic of the tsarist
regime. It was the clearly defined intention of the revolutionaries to eliminate the Church along with the state. Ecclesiastics
of all ranks must share the downfall of the imperial family,
the nobility and the upper *bourgeoisie*.

On the twenty-sixth of October (= eighth of November)
The Second All-Russian Congress of Soviets passed the resolution that "acting on the will of the vast majority of workers,
soldiers, and peasants and in view of the completely successful
revolt of the workers and the garrison in Petrograd, it would
take the authority of government into its own hands." A new
constitution was not adopted until July of the next year and
in this appeared the famous decree on Freedom of Conscience

and on the Separation of the Church from the State and Education for the Church. It read, "For the purpose of securing real freedom of conscience for the workers, the Church is declared separate from the government and the schools from the Church. But freedom for religious and antireligious propaganda is recognized for every citizen."

This decree embodies the basic legal principle on which religion was tolerated and by which it was regulated from 1918–29 when the Fourteenth Congress of Soviets issued a revision in which the article on religion is significantly modified. Instead of "freedom for religious and antireligious propaganda," "freedom in the exercise of religious worship and freedom for antireligious propaganda is recognized for all citizens." Not even citizens were allowed to present the case for religion, although the campaign of the godless remained unimpeded.

The principle of the Constitution both in its original and revised forms was strictly observed, but the picture of its operation must be filled in from a mass of detailed legislation which varied from time to time in its severity. The aim of this legislation is clear: to strip the Church of all the exceptional privileges it enjoyed as an institution with imperial patronage and to place it in that position to which the new government's theory of religion believed it to be entitled. Religion might be enjoyed as a private indulgence on the general principle of civil liberty, but since the official view was that religion was regressive and socially reactionary, its exercise was limited and made as costly as possible.

The law of the state was, however, not the only oppressive force against which the Church must struggle for its existence. The peculiar position of the Communist party in the Soviet state and the large measure of freedom accorded to it in the reorganization of Russian society and the reformation of Russian thought, feeling, and conduct, gave great power and prestige to its antireligious activities. These extended through the whole field of education, not merely in the schools but in museums, recreational centers, theaters, and cinemas, in the Komsomol (the Communist Youth Organization), and in atheistic societies organized and equipped to discredit and combat religion in all its phases. The aims and spirit of the party dominated the new patriotism, conditioned appointments in the civil service, and in the government-controlled industry and on the state and collective farms. In all of these areas of life addiction to religion could be and frequently was used as grounds for discrimination against candidates for any desirable post or occupation, for educational opportunity, or recreational privileges. Life was made narrow and hard for the religious and what was especially important with the young, they were made to feel as outsiders and outcasts who could make no contribution to their country's new era and whose loyalty must be questioned at every turn.

As for the Communists themselves, no ambiguity in their attitude toward religion was tolerated. All party members must abjure religion and subscribe to the campaign of propaganda and discrimination against it, as directed by Lenin in his essay *Socialism and Religion* in 1905.

With the outbreak of the Revolution this became the official policy of the party and was reiterated by Stalin, by the Minister of Education Lunacharskii, by Yaroslavskii, the president of the Atheistical Society, and many others. Lenin's earlier view that religion should be fought only with the weapons of psychological warfare was, however, disregarded and more aggressive measures in keeping with the drift and temper of revolution were adopted. His recommendation in the same essay that "even the mention of the religious attachments of citizens must without question be eliminated from official documents," lost its point when a careful record of such attachments was kept by the party and used consistently to the disadvantage of religious people.

Reliable statistics on the diversion of Church property to secular use are not available, though figures abound. In the report of the Holy Synod to the Finance Committee of the Duma in 1913, "the total income of the monasteries and convents of Russia for the year 1910 was put at 20,627,286 rubles," exclusive of the natural resources of their land, which were not sold but put to community use. Regarding the monasteries of the Russian Church in 1905, Curtis states that the Church

possessed 739,777 desyatinas of land (desyatina = .2.7 acres) in European Russia—an amount equal to 0.2 per cent of that territory. The province having the greatest amount of monastery land was Bessarabia followed in order by Archangel, Tambov, Novgorod, Kherson, Nizhnii Novgorod, and Vladimir. Much of it was waste land, or far northern forest; but enough of it was usable to bring the estimated value of the Church's monastery lands in 1890 to 26,595,690 rubles according to official figures. In 1890 the parish churches of European Russia owned 1,671,198 desyatinas with an estimated worth of 116,195,118 rubles and yielding an annual income of 9,030,204 rubles. By 1905 this average was increased by about 200,000 desyatinas, so that the Church had 0.5 per cent of that part of the country.[1]

Complaints of the wealth and irresponsible luxury of the clergy were persistent and of long standing. Dolgaroukov states that after the death of Peter I, i.e., after his wholesale confiscation of monastic property, "the clergy owned more than 900,000 serfs, a tenth of whom . . . belonged to the famous monastery of S. Sergius near Moscow," and remarks acidly, "The priests and monks lived on the fat of the land, with a superfluity of the goods of this world; abbots of monasteries and bishops especially wallowed in luxury. The eloquent preacher Gideon Krinovskii, archimandrite of the Monastery of S. Sergius and later bishop of Pskov, wore diamond buckles on his shoes!" It is true that the higher clergy continued to enjoy large incomes,

[1] *Op. cit.,* p. 94.

ranging in 1905 from 3,000 (Perm) to 35,000 (Moscow) rubles. Only 7 dioceses yielded less than 5,000 rubles a year; 11 more than 15,000; the majority being 5,000–10,000. The parish clergy in addition to their livings farmed land and collected fees for clerical ministrations. The aggregate was, however, far from impressive. Clerical salaries were not regularly paid by the state until 1893 but in 1895, 12,000,000 rubles were devoted to this purpose. The average norm was fixed by the Holy Synod in 1903 at 300 rubles a year for a priest, 100 for a psalmist, but some went as high as 15,000 rubles and as low as 100. Some received nothing at all from the state. Curtis estimates:

The average income for a village priest in the Russia of 1905 may have been somewhere near 700 rubles. This sum was quite small when compared with the 5,000 and 10,000 rubles and more received by some bishops; and certainly numbers of the priests felt that they were very poorly paid. On the other hand, the average priest was well above the economic level of the average peasant or of the average factory worker.[2]

This situation did not change before the Revolution. From the report of the Holy Synod in 1914 it appears that

there were on the territory of the former Russian Empire 55,173 churches and 29,593 chapels—with 112,629 priests and deacons—550 monasteries and 475 convents with 95,259 inmates. The property and wealth of the church was enormous. It owned 7 million desyatinas of land and many commercial enterprises and houses. Its annual income was estimated to be about 500 million rubles. At the time of the nationalization of the banks its deposits were 8 billion rubles.[3]

Under the Kerensky regime the Church lost control of the schools and there was sporadic but illegal seizure of Church

[2] *Op. cit.*, p. 125.
[3] J. F. Hecker, *Religion and Communism*, p. 294.

lands and other property, but in 1917 everything was swept away and the state took over the title of all Church property, income, and treasure except for the antimensia or squares of cloth enfolding a relic and requisite for the celebration of the Liturgy. In actual value the monastic possessions and Church treasure represented the heaviest loss, but the amount of parish property directed to secular use was formidable. According to Soviet statistics published in 1925 there remained 34,597 congregations in 48 out of 87 government districts; 23,381 Orthodox, 1647 Old Believers, 639 Evangelicals, 141 Roman Catholic, 267 Lutheran, 673 Baptist, 418 Jewish, 1818 Mohammedan and 613 belonging to minor sects. Less than half the districts had an average of 40–50 congregations per 100,000 inhabitants, and in the thinly settled districts of the north and east the number was much smaller. Spinka estimates that 99 per cent of the Orthodox parishes worshiped in churches and almost an equal percentage of Catholics, Lutherans, and Mohammedans had regular places of worship and the Jews were almost as well off. The same report states that 1,003 churches had up to that date been diverted to other uses, schools clubrooms, educational centers, and even lodgings and industrial works. In the following years conditions steadily deteriorated. In 1937 the number of congregations of various sorts in the U.S.S.R. was estimated at 33,839, 15,000 of which applied for registration. There was a great shortage of ministers and the government counted heavily on its restriction of theological education to cripple the conduct of worship. Twenty-eight thousand congregations were said to be without leadership. The income of the surviving congregations had dropped from 50,000,000 in 1914 to a doubtful 10,000,000 in 1937. In an article of this same year based on Soviet press notices Sove reports:

In Belgorod before the Revolution there were three monasteries and twenty-two churches and in the surrounding villages, twenty-five churches. Now there remains one cemetery chapel and in the villages three. (*Izvestia,* August 12, 1936.) In Novgorod out of forty-two churches and three monasteries only fifteen churches remain. Church bells had not been heard in Novgorod for four years (*Antireligioznik,* 1936. No. 1, p. 57.) In the rayon of Kuibishev there were 2,200 churches before the Revolution. Eleven hundred seventy-three were closed. Actually 325 churches functioned (*Pravda,* April 15, 1937).

These figures may be regarded as typical. In 1938 the patriarchal Church under Sergius counted 14,000 parishes. The number of churches open in Moscow dropped from 40 to 25 within a year, 1937–38. The following year 10 more closed. In 1940 the Soviet Press Bureau showed the number of congregations reduced to 30,000 with 8,338 buildings and 52,442 ministers. The Orthodox Church was operating with 4,225 churches, 5,665 priests, 28 bishops and 37 monastic establishments. The reduction in these figures since 1917 ranges from 75 per cent to 90 per cent (Bolshakov).

In spite of these depressing figures religion was far from dead. After the first shock of the Revolution it revived with surprising vigor. Patriarch Tikhon's pleas that the clergy leave politics alone and concentrate their energies on their pastoral duties had its effect. Many bishops returned to their dioceses, the churches were filled with young and old, the traditional holidays were observed. Stratonov claims that "in 1920 church life was restored to its fullness and may even have surpassed the old, prerevolutionary phase. There can be no doubt that the internal growth of awareness of the church within believing Russian society reached a height the equivalent of which had not been seen for 200 years." In 1924 the authors of the atheistic manual *To the Atheistic Youth,* complained that the majority of the peasants still prayed to God for rain and good crops and indulged in other superstitious practices. In 1925 d'Herbigny revisited Moscow and found the majority of churches open and holding services. The Church of the Saviour with its historic frescoes was open in the afternoons to the public as a museum but in the mornings was compulsorily reserved for the visits of worshipers. Among the crowds in the afternoon were those who venerated the icons and kissed the cross in passing. The Church of St. Basil was divided, with the upper story being opened as a museum, the lower chapels reserved for Christian services. The clergy moved freely and undisturbed in the streets in clerical garb. In 1937 Yaroslavskii, the archatheist, held up as a spur to his followers the fact that 80,000,000 believers survived in Russia and in 1940 Nikolsky put the figure 10,000,000 higher, thus embracing one half the total population, and later in the same year an article in *Antireligioznik* declared that half the industrial workers in the towns believed in God and that hardly a thoroughgoing atheist could be found in the villages.

The persistence of religion in the countryside is illustrated by the account of a young political exile who made a covert visit to his people in 1926 and described his experience on Easter Eve.

Four kilometers from our village is an old church belonging to another village but situated in a field. Like the one in our village it has ceased to function. The crosses and bells have been removed from it and the icons have been removed and burned. It has no priest and maintains no services but it has not been occupied, as in our village, as a warehouse and stands empty with unshut doors, open to all and always available. On its walls and ceilings, the old frescoes remain intact. In the day time and in hours of great distress mainly women go there to pray and for a while in quiet and solitude they pass some hours pouring out and relaxing their soul. . . . On Easter Eve 1926 the population of several villages gathered there, some several kilometers away. The old church could not hold them all and the peoples encircled it on all sides in a great throng. In silence, quiet and darkness a crowd of some thousand of people

prayed, wept and awaited midnight. When it came the crowd
chanted, "Christ is risen," and sang the joyous prayer, not dis-
persing, but greeting each other, growing quiet and then beginning
the prayer again until morning. At the first rays of dawn the people
dispersed.[4]

Of much greater significance than the closing of the churches
which, it may be assumed, was contrived for the most part on
the initiative of the Communist party and with government
support, was the psychological warfare waged against religion
by the Communist party, especially among the young. The
weapons chosen were bludgeons rather than rapiers, but the
attack was not made upon a subtle mentality but upon minds
as yet untrained, and won by growing secular appeals as gross
as any employed by irresponsible miracle mongers in earlier
days. The catchwords are those of science instead of theology
but the arguments are usually addressed to the social prejudices,
vanities, and dislikes of simple folk whose receptivity was of
the emotions rather than the mind.

The leaders of the new Russia understood thoroughly that
the success or future of the crusade for atheism depended on
the mobilization of Russian youth. Atheism was therefore
made an essential part of the ethos of young patriots. The
negative side of this campaign was on the whole extremely
successful; the positive apologies for science as opposed to religion depended more on the role of applied science in the
reconstruction of Russian life and industry than upon an attractive presentation of scientific theory. Every effort was made
to inspire the young to be good haters of the past, and this appeal to youthful aggressiveness and destructiveness lent zest to
the whole enterprise.

Numerous manuals for workers in the atheistic movement
were issued by the Communist atheistic societies describing

[4] S. Maslov, *Kolkhoznaya Rossiya*, pp. 93–94. Berlin, 1927.

how confidence in religion could be shattered and faith in science encouraged and sustained. Broad humor and gross parody were favorite devices employed in pamphlets and on placards, in ribald takeoffs of religious festivals and services in which were included orgiastic features reminiscent of the bawdy revels of Peter the Great. From 1922–24 bands of hoodlums from the Komsomol staged these performances in the churches, interrupting the services and insulting the clergy, but public opinion reacted against such indecencies and they were stopped. The point of these sallies was to show that all teachers of religion were cynical and insincere and merely used religion as a means to exploit the masses. The religion of the latter was also declared contemptible because it was illogical and fantastic, the rank growth of uncultivated and uncultured minds. Once the fraud was exposed and the illogicality of faith demonstrated, it was assumed that religious convictions would fade and education would lead liberated minds to the high truths of scientific materialism.

The content of this propaganda is monotonous, unsavory and often childish. A sample may be given from a manual addressed to the Young Atheists in 1924. It begins:

The cultural revolution is proceeding with us much more slowly than the political revolution. The former involves the distinction of those survivals of the old order which were not so clearly or openly related to the sovereignty of capital in the eyes of the workers. Religion occupies a peculiarly important place among such survivals. The whole difficulty lies in the fact that having established religion and made liberal use of it as one of the means for oppressing the working masses, the *bourgeoisie* was able so cleverly to invent the whole system of religion, that religion not only was not regarded by the majority of workers and peasants under its influence, as one of the most powerful instruments of oppression of the *bourgeoisie* but in fact flourished widely as a form of protection against the *bourgeoisie*. . . . The great difficulties which we are

now experiencing with the problem of the struggle with religion
in Bolshevik Russia issues partly from that sentiment, ingrained
for centuries, that has prompted men to seek in religion relief from
earthly sufferings, partly from the abysmal ignorance of our Russian proletariat notably the peasantry. . . . the separation of the
Church from the government, was the first important step on the
road of conflict with religious survivals. Religion became the private
affair of each citizen. But this was only the first step. To reduce
religion to a purely personal way of looking at things, was not a
difficult matter; it was far more difficult to eradicate this seductive
remnant which we have inherited from the old cultural development of the working masses. The Komsomol has devoted itself
with special energy to this task.

Although the pressure of persecution was steady from 1917 to
the outbreak of the war with Germany, it varied in intensity.
The launching of the government's successive economic programs stirred the atheists to fresh endeavors. The famine of
1921 offered the occasion to seize much of the treasure still
left the churches for the conduct of worship. Agitation over
the kulaks or prosperous peasant farmers, when the government's agricultural policy was threatened, brought charges of
liaison between these bourgeois-minded capitalists of the country districts and the dissenting sects. All these served as pre-
texts for fresh confiscations under the wide provisions of the
law.

In the early phases of the famine the patriarch offered the
government assistance in raising funds for relief both in Russian parishes and from Christians abroad to be administered by
the Church authorities. Moscow, however, had no intention of
yielding to the Church the role of provider in a national emergency, much less to permit it the control of funds. The patriarch's
offer was curtly refused. His suggestion that unconsecrated
valuables and even that treasure playing an only indirect role
in the services might be appropriated, was inacceptable and

in February, 1922 Kalinin's decree appeared ordering all objects of value except a minimum requisite for use in the Liturgy be surrendered to the state. Ignoring the government's claim to title in such property, Patriarch Tikhon denounced the new law, declared compliance with it uncanonical, and threatened laymen who handed over consecrated objects to government agents with excommunication, clergy with deposition. Immediate confusion resulted. Many persons were tried and some were executed for obeying the patriarch. The latter was placed under arrest and disaffection among the clergy led him to abdicate his office. The amount realized by these raids has been variously estimated. Government figures reveal 442 kg. of gold; 336,227 kg. of silver; 1,345 kg. of other precious metals; 33,456 diamonds (13.13 carats); 4,414 grams of pearls; 72,383 other precious stones; 20,598 rubles in cash.[5]

It is often pointed out that the government had other reserves to call upon for relief in the famine than the chalices, patens, and icons in use in the churches. The crown jewels alone were valued at $5,000,000 and there were gold reserves sufficient with the help of the American Relief Administration, to meet immediate needs. The Soviet government, however, enjoyed almost universal unpopularity outside Russia at this time and in a world where money not only talked for Russia but raised the only voice which could command a hearing, it was natural that great reluctance was felt in parting with state funds. Furthermore it must be remembered that from the point of view of the ruling party, religious objects were private luxuries put to an asocial, or rather antisocial use by a grudgingly tolerated minority.

The policy of the government was in the highest degree Machiavellian. The confiscations served the double purpose of raising cash and of expressing public contempt for the church. The protests which would inevitably arise from the curtailment

[5] Hecker, *op. cit.*, p. 209, n. 1.

of an already impoverished administration of the sacraments could be so represented as to imply a callous indifference on the part of Christians to the crying need of the populace for food. Foreign assistance, springing, as it usually did, from Christian sentiment and associated with Christian institutions tended to offset this impression and was resented. A cold reception was accorded to the work of the A.R.A. and acceptance of aid from the Pope's Commission on Relief for Russian Children was even more frigid.

The launching of the first Five Year Plan was accompanied by an orgy of persecution occasioned by the famine. In 1922 the first atheistical publication of note, the weekly *Bezbozhnik,* began to circulate and in the following year the atheistical organizations got under way and began to extend their influence to education, recreation and the army. Meanwhile the Church had more or less set its affairs in order. The Patriarch Tikhon was released from prison and his position rehabilitated. In 1927 Sergius succeeded in establishing a temporary Patriarchal Holy Synod and his negotiations with the Soviet authorities continued to be marked with increasing success.

These developments did not pass unnoticed by the atheists. The second Five Year Plan offered an occasion for renewed attacks upon the Church. Conferences were called, new forms of propaganda devised, lagging enthusiasm was stirred and every occasion seized for closing churches. It was rumored that the atheists had their own five year plan which was guaranteed to stamp out religion completely while contributing to the political morale and economic efficiency of the government's program.

In the program for antireligious propaganda adopted April, 1926 by the Party Conference on Antireligious Propaganda and by the Central Committee of the Communist Party great sagacity in planning the campaign was shown. A thorough understanding of the problem and gradual patient action was recommended. The nature of religion must be grasped, its objective role and subjective power must be studied, and the strategy of atheism must be adjusted to the actual functioning of religion in different social and economic circumstances. The zeal of the workers, however, tolerated no such caution. It was more fun to parody religion than to investigate it and any stick was good enough to beat a priest. The editors of the manual quoted above ingenuously acknowledge that the early efforts to discredit religion did not meet with unqualified success. Mistakes were made and the youthful crusaders against God became more preoccupied with the form than with the substance of the campaign. The theatricals proved more attractive than their deeper meaning and purpose. "Mistakes were made" and the believers were angered but not convinced. Nevertheless in the mind of the leaders this phase was not a waste. "The working youth revealed their atheistical bent," and "a heavy blow was dealt clerical bigotry and hypocrisy"; "it was made evident in whose interests the priests were working and it was pointed out that few people had considered what God must be like, if his representatives on earth were such swindlers or indeed if he existed at all."

Some idea of this kind of propaganda may be gained from one of the plays included in the manual and designed for production as amateur theatricals by youth groups in the recreation centers. The cast includes a priest, an old woman, the prophet Moses, two Jews, the God Elohim, the devil, a Soviet boy scout, an officer of the Komsomol, and a chorus of angels. The scene opens with a dialogue between the old woman whose coarse humor and broad dialect underline her ignorance in accepting religion. She asks for an explanation of the creation of the world in six days according to Scripture. The priest begins to read the story in Genesis but the scene is transferred to Mt. Sinai and the priest and the old woman, together with the angels, serve as a kind of Greek chorus to connect the action. Moses appears with the tables of the Law and is confronted by two Jews who are sent by their people to find Moses. The latter instructs them to say he is in conversation with God. One Jew says that the people want Moses to show them God and explain his significance. Moses explains that anyone who sees God will be blinded and that they must cover their faces. He then improvises a conversation with God, changing his voice appropriately to the two roles. The burden of the message is that God created the world and that the account is to be found in Genesis. The priest then begins to read the sacred text, whereupon the scene changes to heaven.

There occurs a long section in which creation is enacted. Much is made of the beginning in dark chaos for which neither God nor the angels can give satisfactory explanation. The devil appears and suggests that conversation would be easier if there were light, so God creates light. The successive acts of creation are performed all at the suggestion of the devil who plays the role of common sense against the blundering stupidity of God. From time to time the boy scout puts in an appearance and expounds in a pedantic and most unscoutlike fashion the divergences between Genesis I and II, thus discrediting the whole action but injecting a new note of skepticism.

When the creation of man is announced there is a sudden interruption. The young Komsomolets advances from the wings and shouts:

Who wrote this scenario? Come on now, show me the one who wrote this scenario.

Voice from the back timidly: He isn't in the club at present.

Komsomolets: Ah! no! Well, we'll do without him. (Addressing the audience.) Please tell me, comrades, what is this all about?

Priest (to old woman): And who would this be?

Old woman: This is the top leader of the Youth Groups. The other one was a leader but this one is higher up. Their field marshal.

Komsomolets: It appears from this play that God created everything at the suggestion of the devil, for some reason or other. He created the grass because there was nowhere to sit down. He created the stars to decorate that old wooden firmament, and finally he tried to create man to rule over the beasts. There's nothing like this in the Bible, comrades. According to the Bible, comrades, God created everything for no reason at all visible or invisible except that you might live well. And it couldn't be otherwise for primitive imagination created God. Yes comrades, God didn't create man but man, primitive man, created God. But swindling priests like Moses or this priest here used these facts to oppress the illiterate, ignorant workers. The world was created quite differently. The world was created not in six or seven days but in many, many millions of years.

Priest (in a rage): But tell me, sir comrade, whatever created itself? And you say man descended from a monkey (winking at the audience).

Old Woman: Holy Mother of God!

Komsomolets: The world and life on the earth and man, all these are parts of one whole. This whole is called: the eternal cosmic motion in space. But let us see, Father priest, how your God created man?

God (morosely): Let us create man in our image and likeness. . . .

(*From an opening emerges an almost naked hairy man.*)

Chorus of angels (to the tune of *Karavai*):
>   Man, O man, immortal never
>   Be our willing slave forever.

Komsomolets: What's this? A man or a woman.

God: I don't know.

Komsomolets: Yes, comrades. In the first chapter of the Bible nothing is said of this. Most likely this creature was sexless. But in the second chapter of the Book of Genesis, it is said that man was created first and then woman from his rib. The one piece of nonsense contradicts the other. And this is quite intelligible. Moses did not write the Bible by himself. He may never even have existed. The learned representatives of the classes in power wrote the Bible from one tribe to another, from one generation to another. They added one thing to another, inventing combinations of folk tales and fables. . . . But the really offensive thing, comrades, is the fact that among us now in the Soviet Union are people who believe in this nonsense. They have before their eyes the splendid achievements created by the liberated proletariat. The proletariat says, "Let there be light," and electric light, shines not only in the towns but in the dark, downtrodden villages. The proletariat says, "Let there be plants in the dusty cities," and on the squares rise green paths and garden plots. The proletariat says, "We shall create a warrior equipped from head to foot with science," and this man already exists; he is already growing up, he is around us, he takes the place of old and young. (*During this speech, God, the devil and the angels disappear from the scene. The boy scout comes out from behind the lectern and stands beside the Komsomolets.*) And the proletariat says, "Be ready to take our places, to destroy the old world, to break the accursed yoke of capital and to build a new world for a new free humanity. Be prepared, comrade, eventually to subdue nature to yourself, to dominate it and compel it to serve your aims. Be prepared to conquer blind destiny, fate, providence. Be prepared to conquer death itself, to subject the movements of the earth to your control and after that all motion in universal space." And now what does the young comrade have to say in reply?

Scout (saluting): Always prepared.

Komsomolets: And you, black face, when will you perish from our city? Only when there shall be no more illiterates in our towns and villages. Then you will flee to hell along with your Elohim and devil and all spirits clean and unclean!

Obviously the success of such a production could not depend on its bookish monologues on Biblical criticism nor on its vapid allusions to the importance of natural science. Its invective would undoubtedly stir latent iconoclasm, especially in the circles to which this kind of presentation was addressed, but even the old formula that religion was an instrument of oppression in the hands of the aristocracy and *bourgeoisie* must have lost some of its excitement once it was clear that there were no longer hands to wield it. Not even the hysteria of propaganda could render the pathetic remnants of organized religion a plausible counterrevolutionary threat. The strength of the piece lies in its appeal to the forward movement of the Revolution itself and in its references and achievements of which every level-headed Russian was justly proud: electric installations, cleaner and more attractive surroundings especially for the working men in the towns, the rising level of education and the growing control and exploitation of Russia's vast natural resources, the management of which in the past had been so neglected and bungled.

The historic association of religion in Russia with obscurantism, the suppression of education and the thwarting of enterprise worked as effectively here to the disadvantage of the Church as its association with a tyrranous absolutist state had worked against it in the political sphere. Here, as in the struggle of the intelligentsia with Orthodoxy, there was no middle ground, no working liberalism. The pressure of arbitrary privilege was not relaxed in the face of large national tasks, greater demands upon a greater number, and of the need for more equity in the adjustment of profits to labor and of rights to responsibilities. In spite of its coarseness and unsavoriness, this kind of antireligious propaganda contained moral conviction. Plain facts of injustice and inefficiency had spoken plainly to men's minds and consciences and they struck brutally, fanatically, and without due consideration at the institutions which tolerated and encouraged these social evils. The larger view was for the time being lost; autocratic injustice yielded to revolutionary intolerance; the pendulum of history swung far before reaching equilibrium again.

The attack on religion, however, in spite of its moral strength and physical violence was essentially inadequate. A generation has not yet passed since the outbreak of the Revolution and its avowed objective, the extermination of religion from Russian life, is a recognized failure. There has been much destruction and alienation of Church property and widespread disaffection from the Church, especially among the young, as a result of ideological and social pressure of various kinds. Religion is, however, not dead but rising again.

The outstanding weakness in the attack appears to have been the failure to understand the nature of religion as a psychological force either in the individual or in society. An argument may be cracked but an experience cannot be shattered by a syllogism, and the intellectual onslaught on religion suffered not only from its patent ineptitude but from its ignorance of where the roots of religion lie. In treating theological tradition as if it were current scientific theory which needed only to be refuted on the surface in order to be discredited, Soviet critics accomplished little more than the pruner who cuts the leaves and surplus branches from the treetops. The result in the long run was to encourage a more healthy growth.

The hostile criticism of the Church drove home not without pain, but with effect, and paved the way for a re-estimate of the indestructible resources of religion, the intellectual and moral reserves of the Church, the strength and consolations of an informed devotion. A new phase in Russian theology opened and from it stemmed a new apologetic. Conditions of censorship under the Soviet state have prevented a clear picture of this development from emerging, just as the imperial censorship drove the religious liberalism of the nineteenth and early twentieth centuries underground. Some idea, however, of what has been won by much suffering and heroic endurance and perseverance can be gained from the essays in *The Truth About Religion in Russia,* from the collection of patriarchal and archiepiscopal pronouncements recently issued by the patriarchate in Moscow, from the writings of the more liberal theologians of the Emigration notably in Paris, and from the Orthodox press in this country.

In surveying this dark period in the history of the Russian Church, it is evident that two conservative forces operated to avert complete disaster. The first was the extraordinary tenacity of religion as a force in Russian life and its vitality in the face of determined opposition on the part of all who were successfully leading the nation in other spheres of national interest. The second was the patience, resourcefulness, and initiative of the newly re-established patriarchate. With the collapse of the tsarist regime the visible head of the Church disappeared and with him its chief executive, the High Procurator. The whole administration of the Church threatened to disintegrate and chaos would inevitably have resulted if the council of Moscow (1917) had not acted immediately to preserve discipline and place it in nonpolitical hands. This was the point of the re-establishment of the patriarchate.

The council of Moscow was the one long promised by the tsars but always indefinitely postponed. After the Russo-Japanese war when all sorts of tendencies toward decentralization were at work, Nicholas II went as far as appointing a preliminary committee to consider the organization and agenda of such a council, but the project was shelved on the insistence of Pobedonostsev. Taking advantage of the freedom accorded by the Kerensky regime, the Church moved on its own and convened the council August 15, 1917. The proceedings dragged but on October 30, 1917 the patriarchate was restored. On November 4 the authority of the patriarchate was defined. The *sobor* retained supreme authority in ecclesiastical affairs and the patriarch was declared *primus inter pares* and responsible to the council. Three candidates were nominated of whom Anthony Khrapovitsky had the majority of votes, but the final selection was made by lot and Tikhon, who had the least support in the elections, was taken and enthroned on November 5.

The character and abilities of Tikhon have been variously

estimated. At the time of his election he was metropolitan of Moscow and in earlier days had been rector of the theological seminary at Kazan, bishop of Lublin and of Alaska and the Aleutian Islands which included jurisdiction over the United States. Through his initiative the latter was transformed into an archdiocese of which he was the first incumbent. In 1907 he became archbishop of Yaroslav and in 1913 archbishop of Wilno. He was made metropolitan of Moscow June 19, 1917. Politically the patriarch was a conservative and loyal tsarist. After the tsar's abdication and detention Tikhon is said to have sent him the Sacred Host for his communion. He bitterly resented the Bolshevik attack on Orthodoxy and spoke out with great vigor in a pronouncement both against the government's religious policy and against its termination of the war with Germany, for which he was never forgiven. He was, however, clear-sighted enough to see that if the Church was to survive it must play a strictly nonpolitical role and he urged his clergy to keep their hands out of politics.

It may be conjectured that the attitude of his brother priests rather than the pressure of a godless state broke Tikhon's spirit. In 1922 at the insistence of Krasnitskii, Vvedenskii and their friends he abdicated and for three years the life of the Church hung in the balance. His ecclesiastical opponents split into factions representing various degrees of political radicalism and united only by a common trust in expediency rather than precedent, experimentation rather than discipline, and opinion rather than dogma. These groups of which the so-called Living Church was the most powerful convened a synod at Moscow in 1923, without a vestige of canonical right, denounced the patriarch as a counterrevolutionary, deprived him of his orders and monastic status and declared "hereafter Patriarch Tikhon is layman Basil Belavin."

It is impossible here to pursue this painful chapter of schism in detail and the story has been told many times.[6] Once again we are confronted with the impact of two forces launched from extreme positions and meeting head on. It must be emphasized that even after the Revolution the liberal clergy had no effective representation in Church affairs. Tikhon's leadership at first had drawn the Church away from the current social trend and dissociated it from the new world of the Revolution. Many of the more intelligent and progressive clergy believed this stand to be both false and inexpedient. Behind this attitude was a larger background of liberal thought and attitude on many questions of theology, science, and morals which had been suppressed but not extinguished in the seminaries and by the hierarchy in power. The Living Church and its allies represented a belated outburst of liberalism on all fronts and a great soreness at the exclusion of the Church from the forward movement of Russian life. It was this feature which gave to the Living Church its strength and appeal and evoked sympathy even in England and America with its cause.

By 1925, however, all these movements had failed. The reason for their failure was that their roots did not strike deeply enough into Russian life. To the average believer the patriarchate had again become the symbol of unity, authenticity, and integrity and with characteristic caution the religious sentiment clung to the old attachments. Most Russians preferred to divide their allegiance between a secular state and the Church of their fathers, rather than attempt a hasty accommodation of old loyalties to new and untried forces. Never has the unifying power of tradition asserted itself so instinctively and powerfully as in Russian religious behavior between 1923–25.

It was natural that the Bolsheviks should take pleasure in the divided councils of churchmen and should manipulate the schisms to their own end. In the long run, however, the Living

[6] Cf. P. Miliukov "Outlines of Russian Culture," Part I: *Religion and the Church* (Philadelphia: University of Pennsylvania Press, 1942), p. 168.

Church offered no advantages over Orthodoxy to the Communist politicians. In spite of its lip service to socialism the Living Church rested on the fundamental premises of religion and therefore received no sustained support from the state or party. Stepanov expressed this official view when he wrote:

We do not doubt that among the members of the Living Church will appear some simple-minded people who will imagine that scientific Communism is equivalent to the ideal of pure Christianity. The misfortune of the Russian clergy is that it is several centuries behind. In these days "religious communism" is an incident of little importance in the larger movement under the hoisted scientific Communist flag. . . . The Communist party must not criticize the old Church for fear of strengthening the Living Church and must not criticize the Living Church for fear of raising up a more radical church. The only effective criticism is to turn the masses from any church, any clergy, and any religion.

The date for Tikhon's trial had been set by the government as June 15, 1923 and cards of admission already issued when the patriarch was allowed an opportunity to retract his former utterances against the government, be released, and return to his duties. In a statement published in facsimile in the Bolshevik press Tikhon admitted the error of his antagonism to the Soviet power, formally recognized it as the *de facto* government of Russia and called upon the faithful to support it loyally. He moved immediately to the Don Monastery and resumed his patriarchal functions. His first important act was to denounce the Living Church and declare all its acts void. He appealed to all those who had fallen away to return. One of those who responded and did public penance for their defection was the future Patriarch Sergius.

The rigors of the revolutionary years, the strain of public condemnations and imprisonment proved too much for Tikhon's health; he died April 7, 1925. Metropolitan Peter Krutitskii took over the administration of the Church as locum tenens but on account of disagreements with the authorities was exiled to Siberia within less than a year. He was succeeded by Sergius, later metropolitan of Moscow.

The new locum tenens proved to be the man of the hour. Broad experience in Church affairs at home and abroad had equipped him for a role which demanded a rare combination of the qualities of leadership and diplomacy. He had been rector of the Ecclesiastical Academy in St. Petersburg, rector of the embassy church in Athens, chairman of the educational committee of the Holy Synod, active in the mission field in Japan, archbishop of Finland, metropolitan of the sees of Vladimir and Nizhnii Novgorod and in April, 1934 was made metropolitan of Moscow and Kolomna. His lapse into the Living Church was an indication of liberal social views and unlike his predecessors he viewed contemporary events in Russia in perspective and ungrudgingly estimated real progress at its worth. His view of the Communist state was technically identical with his predecessors'. He recognized it as the *de facto* government and so ordained of God (Romans 13:5). His pastoral concern and social vision, however, opened his eyes to the necessity of establishing and maintaining an integral connection between the Church and the new social and political order. In his relations with the Bolsheviks he was adroit but tenacious of his point. Where Tikhon had failed, he succeeded in having the Church registered as a corporate body. More surprising he obtained permission for a *sobor* to be held at which he was elevated from locum tenens to the patriarchate. His enthronement was the occasion of solemn and widespread rejoicing at home and abroad. Before his death he extracted a concession from the government to open a theological seminary for the training of Orthodox priests, an amazing reversal of earlier policy which proposed by closing such institutions gradually to deprive the faithful of all ministrations. A state commission for the regulation of Orthodox affairs was also appointed. After some years of silence it has recommended extention of religious education to which ten years ago no responsible Bolshevik would have listened, has permitted an All-Russian *sobor* and the election of a new patriarch, Alexei. More than one factor contributed to these remarkable changes, but without the initiative and persistence of Sergius it is unlikely any would have actually taken place.

In estimating the work of the restored patriarchate it should be remembered that it cannot have been an easy venture to have risked the future of Russian Orthodoxy on the recognition of the Bolshevik state, the avowed hostility of whose leaders had caused so much damage and suffering in Orthodoxy in the early years of its power. The favorable interpretation recently given to the decree on "Liberty of Conscience" in the Constitution is hardly reconcilable with that placed upon it earlier by state officials in their dealings with Christian persons and property. The antireligious educational policy of the government was not confined to attacks on the old association of Church and State, but also upon theology and the practice of religion as radically opposed to the fundamental social and cultural views of the government. The insight into Russian mentality and the foresight of a certain return to the values of religion indicate the kind of vision by which history is made and directed. The more unpromising the situation in the twenties is envisaged, the more credit accrues to the astuteness and judgment of Tikhon and Sergius. In the complex of decisions which determined their course, a deep and pastoral sense of responsibility toward the actual religious needs of the Russian people predominated. These common folk could find no refuge in the ivory towers of foreign capitals nor be patronized by the exiled courts of grand dukes and princes. Whether loyal or disloyal to the ancient creed, the Russian people were the flock of Russian pastors, the Church of Tikhon, Peter

Sergius, and Alexei holds the shepherds who stayed on the ground to care for them. The decision to do this was dangerous and in the eyes of many wrongheaded, but it required not only the courage of conviction but also a single-minded concern for the care of souls.

Chapter V

THE REVIVAL OF ORTHODOXY

ON JUNE 22, 1941 HITLER BROKE HIS TREATY with Russia (August 31, 1939) and the German armies without warning crossed the border and proceeded to occupy the country. With characteristic speed and competence the invading armies overran Central and Southern Russia, struck north toward Moscow and besieged Leningrad. The immediate objectives were Ukrainian grain and minerals and Caucasian oil, but the ultimate goal was to smash the military power of the Soviet state and exploit all its resources for German gain.

The details of the occupation are preserved not only in the official collections of documents and photographs which the Soviet government is now publishing but in the war literature, mainly short stories, which transform typical incidents into living tragedy and present the drama of emotions behind the sordid events of conquest.

One such story thus describes the terror which the first impact of the German forces produced: "It may have been only a minute or even less, in all just an instant, but it seemed to many an eternity and to go through it insuperably difficult, as to go through death itself."

The record of the horrors of the German occupation is extensive, monotonous and undescribably ugly. It is, however, important for our purpose to reconstruct the general scene in order to estimate its effect on the religious sensibilities of the

Russian people. Occupation was invariably accompanied by plundering and this did not confine itself to food and warm clothing which were snatched from persons on the streets and dug out of closets and trunks, but included anything to which a German private might take a fancy to keep or find amusing to destroy. In the town of Lyalovo in the Solnechnogorskii rayon of the Moscow district the citizens declared in an official deposition:

On November 28, 1941 German troops invaded our town and began to rob the peaceful inhabitants. The Fascists stripped the collective-farmers of their felt and leather boots and warm clothing right on the street. They also plundered dwellings. The Germans took from P. A. Belov his felt boots on the street and stole a second pair of footwear found in his house. From E. G. Kornysheva's the Fascists took her husband's felt boots and three quilted coats. The thieves took children's blouses, sewing machines and even cattle troughs. From Citizenness Kornysheva they took a sewing machine and all her provisions. From Citizenness Belova the Fascists took a sack of rye which they fed their horses. The Fascists went through the houses looking for baked bread and meal; they opened trunks and stripped them of their contents.

On the occupation of the town the Germans drove all the women into the church and the men into the co-operative store, in order to plunder the dwellings more freely. They kept the population in this manner for eight days. On leaving the town the Germans burned thirty-eight houses. We should also mention that the German soldiers wore summer coats and boots and under their coats they stuffed various stolen articles. They were literally crawling with lice and the Germans compelled us to delouse the clothing of the German soldiers.[1]

This account is confirmed by a letter written by a German soldier to his parents:

[1] *Dokumenty obvinyayut*, p. 507. Moscow, 1943.

My dear parents:

We always have enough to eat. If there is any lack, we simply take a duck or a goose. When we are in town we eat more than we need. In the morning a litre of milk, for dinner and in the evening a whole goose, in the evening again a litre of milk and four or five eggs. We go to the local populace and take eggs and milk.

. . . Yes I can already say many things in Russian. We have much meat; there is much cattle and many pigs in this neighborhood. We have only to take them. We're the kind that take everything we want. We are never hungry.[2]

It may be objected that these acts were the products of local emergency or irresponsible aggression, but the evidence is cumulative and the German orders captured and now published by the Russians leave no doubt about the policy of the German High Command. An order from the commander of the Seventy-eighth Division of the German Infantry Division in retreat on December 24, 1941, at 6:30 A.M. reads:

The position of the enemy and the necessity of protecting reserves make a retreat of the army unavoidable. Details of the retreat: See to it you take with you only objects essential for living and fighting. Destroy everything else. Unless it can be taken with you destroy all valuable material found in the cottages like glass, stoves, etc. Blow up the cottages. On the burning of the towns consult the enclosed. [The enclosure gives minute instructions for the systematic destruction of towns, villages and civilian property by sappers, mines and fire and concludes:] This order must under no circumstances fall into the hands of the enemy. In any case this document should be destroyed.[3]

Local orders for requisitioning food were accompanied by threats to burn homes.

[2] *Ibid.*, p. 142.
[3] *Ibid.*, p. 48.

Threats of this kind were no mere gestures. Specific acts of disobedience to army orders or to military authority in any form were, as might be expected, severely punished, but the exaggerated brutality with which the civilian population was handled was designed to create that feeling of terrified submissiveness which the German army had sought everywhere to create and which it found most useful for its purposes. Diaries and letters found on German prisoners vividly confirm the theory behind the acts of savagery committed. One soldier wrote in his diary:

I, Heinrich Tivel, have set as my goal for this war to destroy indiscriminately 250 Russians, Jews, Ukrainians. If each soldier killed a like number, we would destroy Russia in a month. We Germans would get everything. In accordance with the Fuehrer's order I call on all Germans to realize this aim.[4]

Another reflecting on the mass shooting of eighty-two suspects in a detention camp, wrote:

Is it true, the more you kill the easier it gets? I remember my childhood. Was I affectionate? I hardly think so. One must be hardhearted. In the end we shall destroy the Russians; they are Asiatics. The world should be grateful to us.[5]

How clear an echo of official sentiment the tone of this letter is, appears from a singularly revealing memorandum on the general conduct of the Russian campaign by no less a person than General von Reichenau. A copy was sent with the express commendation of Hitler to the local commands. It reads:

MEMORANDUM ON THE CONDUCT OF TROOPS IN THE EASTERN THEATER

With regard to the behavior of troops toward the Bolshevist system a considerable lack of clarity still prevails. The essential aim

[4] *Ibid.*, p. 140.
[5] *Ibid.*, p. 140.

of the campaign against the Jewish-Bolshevik system is the complete annihilation of the power and the elimination of the Asiatic influence in the European cultural area.

In this connection problems arise even for the troops which go beyond the hitherto exclusively military training. In the eastern theater the soldier is not only a fighter according to the rules of warfare but also the bearer of an inexorable racial idea and the avenger of all the bestialities which have been perpetrated on Germans and the peoples related to them.

The soldier must therefore have a complete understanding of the necessity for a harsh but just retribution on the Jewish sub-humanity (*Untermenschentum*). This retribution has the further purpose of nipping in the bud uprisings in the rear of the (advancing) German army which as we know from experience are generally stirred up by Jews.

The fight against the enemy behind the front lines has not yet been taken seriously enough. Crafty and horrible Patriots (*Partisani*) and perverse women are still treated as prisoners of war and guerillas and tramps dressed half in uniform or in civilian dress are treated like respectable soldiers and delivered to the prisoners' camps. Captured Russian officers state derisively that Soviet agents circulate undiscovered in the streets and frequently eat in German mess-halls. Such behavior on the part of our troops can only be explained by complete thoughtlessness. It is therefore high time that the officers evoked among their men a realization of the present struggle.

Provisioning of the local population and war prisoners who are not in the employ of the German army is as misconceived an act of humanity as gifts of cigarettes and bread. The soldier has no business to give the enemy things that the homeland dispenses with at a great sacrifice and the administration brings to the front under the greatest difficulties, even though these things be taken from booty (appropriated in the locality). This is a necessary part of our concern. The Soviets have often set buildings on fire during their retreat. The troops have an interest in putting out fires only when necessary supplies for the troops must be salvaged. Otherwise the disappearance of the symbols of former Bolshevik rule even in the form of buildings is a part of the struggle for annihilation. Neither historical nor artistic considerations play any role in the eastern theater of operations. The administration issues the necessary directions for the preservation of important defensive raw materials and centers of production. The thorough disarming of the population in the rear of the fighting troops is of the first importance in view of the long and vulnerable lines of supply. When possible, weapons and munition taken as booty are to be hidden and guarded. If the combat conditions do not permit this, the weapons and munition are to be rendered unusable. If the use of weapons by individual Patriots is demonstrable, the situation is to be handled with the utmost severity. This applies also to the male population who might be in a position to prevent or warn of attacks. The neutrality of substantial elements apparently hostile to the Soviets, which derives from a tenative attitude, must yield to a clear decision in favor of co-operation against Bolshevism. Otherwise no one can complain for being regarded and treated as an adherent of the Soviet system. The terror of German reprisals must be made greater than the threat of itinerant Bolshevik survivors.

Apart from all political considerations about the future, the soldier has two duties to perform: (1) the complete extermination of the Bolshevik heresy, of the Soviet state and its armed forces; (2) the merciless annihilation of perverse craftiness and terrorism and the insurance by this means of the life of the German army in Russia.

Only in this way will we do justice to our historic task of liberating the German people for all time from the Asiatic-Jewish danger.

SUPREME COMMANDER VON REICHENAU
General Field Marshal [6]

It is improbable that von Reichenau was the author of this fanatical composition or that more than his signature was required of him by the Ministry of Propaganda which produced it. The curious mixture of military regulations and ideological fervor, however, attests the extent to which the German army

[6] *Ibid*. (German text), p. 93.

in Russia were fighting on the principles and for the program of National Socialism. The vitriolic references to the Jews and the spiteful description of the Russians as "Asiatics" are unmistakable echos of Herr Rosenberg's racial theory. In a set of official instructions in similarly lyrical vein the German soldier is enjoined:

Morning, noon and night think always of the Fuehrer. Let no other thoughts disturb you; know that he is thinking and acting for you. You have only to act and fear nothing, for you, a German soldier, are invincible. Not a bullet, not a bayonet will affect you, nerves nor heart nor pity, for you are made of German iron. After the war you will rediscover a new spirit and a serene heart for your children, your wife and for mighty Germany. But now act resolutely, unhesitatingly for mighty Germany.

A German cannot be cowardly. When it goes hard with you, think of the Fuehrer and act resolutely. They will all perish from your blows. Remember Germany's greatness and victory. For your personal glory you must kill exactly one hundred Russians. This is a just equation, for one German is equal to one hundred Russians. You have neither heart nor nerves for these things are not needful for war. Crush in yourself pity and compassion. Kill every Russian and Soviet. Do not hesitate if it be an old man or woman, a little girl or boy who is in your way. Kill and you will save yourself from ruin, you will make your future family safe and you will be famous forever.

There is not a force in the world that can withstand German pressure. We shall bring the whole world to its knees. A German is an absolute master of the world. You will decide the fate of England, Russia and America. You, a German, will, as befits a German, destroy every living creature which puts itself in your way. Think always of the exalted one, the Fuehrer, and you will win. Neither bullet nor bayonet can touch you. Tomorrow the whole world will be on its knees at your feet.

A feeble but nonetheless often utilized instrument of psychological warfare was the German claim to be Christian crusaders in Russia, undertaking to restore to the Russian people the consolations of religion. Placards bearing edifying inscriptions were prominently posted in the occupied towns. After a journey of inspection through the districts of Moscow and Kalinin, the archpriest Smirnov reported:

> During their advance on Moscow the Germans issued at Klin in the house-museum of P. I. Tchaikovsky, after the devastation effected there, a pamphlet with the title "God with us." A characteristic and regular attempt of the Germans is to sanctify their whole campaign on Russian soil with the name of God and to cover and justify with that name all their indescribable barbarous acts by calling them a "crusade on Russia."

This probably was the least successful device for political camouflage attempted by the German office of propaganda. After the years of cynical outrages on Catholics, Protestants, and Jews in Germany and occupied countries, the outside world was not likely to be inspired by the thought of Hitler as the champion of religion and in Russia the behavior of the German troops soon disillusioned any Christians, who hoped that the Bolshevik hostility toward the Church would be superceded by the protection and encouragement of the war lords under the New Fascist Order. No exceptions were made to the general reign of terror in the interest of religion. Church property and the modest private possessions of the clergy were subject to the same ruthless violation as those of the rest of the population.

So far from enjoying the special consideration of the invading armies, the churches were a favorite butt of gratuitous attack. Among many cases reported by Smirnov,[7] the village church of Peshka near Solnechnogorsk on the Leningrad highway was first plundered, then turned into a stable for the German cavalry and finally demolished. In the village of Chasknikovo

[7] These were published in *Pravda o religii v Rossii*. Moscow, 1942.

in the Chimkinski rayon of the Moscow district the Germans robbed the parish church of all its sacred objects, forced its priest to flee into the woods in winter cold without boots, and on the retreat from Moscow blew up the church building. In the village of Yemelyanovo in the Katiniv district the church was burned and as a preliminary the troops amused themselves by shooting to pieces the icons and pictures. The village priest of Volovnika in the Klimkii rayon wrote to the patriarch on March 20, 1942:

My church in Volovnika has been wrecked and burned almost to its foundations. The Germans, the new "crusaders," first plundered it then turned it into an ammunition dump and near it used to execute our Red Army soldiers. The war has been savage and for our church has ended bitterly. When I learned what the Germans had done to our church, I hurried over to remove the antimension and the Blessed Sacrament but when I arrived the battle was already in progress and I could not even get into the church. For that matter, the Germans would probably not have allowed me. While I was away, the workers' settlement was set on fire and the house in which I lived was burned. All my books were burned, my records and notes. The Germans had made away with my few belongings.

The demolition of sacred buildings as well as historical and cultural monuments appears to have been a normal procedure in the general plan of occupation. It is not surprising that the German "crusade" failed to carry conviction.

It is a remarkable feature of the Russian campaign that the Germans received relatively little help from collaborationists. No men of note and influence like Quisling, Laval, and Antonescu offered the support of numerous followers to the German cause. There were, however, collaborationists: small men, frustrated bureaucrats, embittered enthusiasts for the old regime, and ecclesiastical adventurers. The Germans anticipated this and the military orders gave instructions to exploit to the full any civil or religious differences among the civilian population. The emergence of this hidden force in village life on the arrival of the German troops is vividly described in a Ukrainian short story, *The Black Cross* by Petro Panch.[8] The village school teacher arrives home from a short journey to find the occupation in full swing.

Elena Pavlova shivered. It was terrible to think that the door would open shortly and those whom she had so often described to the children as the most fearful enemies would come rushing in. They would destroy everything for which she had lived and in which she had taken delight. One thing she understood clearly: neither in this room nor through the windows outside did the Soviet Ukraine exist any more, only black crosses and soldiers with skulls on their caps. Everything that was familiar and dear to her had left with the Red Army; she was left alone with these beasts. It was sickeningly dreary and empty. She slipped on a warm shawl but the feverish chill would not stop. The tank opposite the window leaped forward firing its guns; like a dog on a chain it also clanked with chains. It barked furiously at the Red Army which was retreating but was in no hurry. The Bolsheviks took a step backwards, struck their opponents a head blow, and then took another step. German tanks were advancing but fear compelled them with its mighty fists to keep their distance and to hop with impotent rage. Time after time they discharged their shells which went roaring like dogs after their prey.

Through the window peered the face of Ivan Sidorovich, a bookkeeper at the collective farm, a quiet, conscientious man. Elena Pavlova sighed with relief; she was not alone in this situation and for comfort even death is red. They would think up something. But behind the accountant flashed bayonets. "That's the way it's got to be," thought Elena Pavlova. . . . "They've arrested Sidorovich and they've come for me."

Suddenly the thought ceased to frighten her; she only wished the whole thing might be over quickly. As though bidding it farewell,

[8] Published in Russian in the collection *Gnyevnoye Slovo*, p. 46. Moscow, 1942. The English rendering is mine.

she glanced around her room. This was still her own world, the Soviet world. From the wall Lenin smiled paternally down at her. The Fascists had begun to stream into the building and she instinctively put up her hand to cover it as if she were protecting someone. Photographs, pictures and books stood in a row. The whole room in short shone with the Soviet light and it was impossible to shield or protect it or even to destroy it herself.

Her hand fell powerless. Looking at her mother, Elena Pavlova smiled bitterly. She was silently hurrying about the room, hiding Mark's little suits as best she could. Tears flowed down her wrinkled cheeks like heavy rain. Behind her Mark wandered about like a shadow. Suddenly he turned to his mother and said, "Grandma says our life has gone to pieces. Is that true, mamma? Are the Germans coming?" Elena Pavlova threatened him fearfully with her hand and listened. Along the corridor heavy steps sounded. She drew herself up, arranged the shawl over her shoulders and sat down at the table. She drew little Mark to herself and placed her hand on his blond head. "To exist is not the same thing as to live. It is necessary to bite," she said seriously.

The door crashed open and Ivan Sidorovich's lean, blotched face emerged from the black gap. He smiled ironically and Elena Pavlova blinked at him. It seemed as if she were surprised that it was Ivan Sidorovich but he was in point of fact actually entering the room and was smiling a malevolent kind of smile. Behind him, like tin soldiers who couldn't bend their knees, the Germans entered and stood behind him. Elena Pavlova covered her face with her hand; the Fascists stood in the room.

"Didn't you want to leave or didn't you have time, Elena Pavlova," Ivan Sidorovich asked insinuatingly. Elena looked at him, opened her eyes wide and was silent. "That means, you didn't have time. Don't look so surprised; I've waited twelve years for this. Give the soldiers some milk. It is necessary to have done with these things forever." He struck the portraits of the Leader with his stick and dashed them to the floor. The soldiers glanced around and began to talk rapidly about something.

"Milk, do you hear?" Ivan Sidorovich commanded and his whole face changed immediately. His back straightened, he squared his shoulders, he drew up his small head on his scrawny neck as if he had before him instead of the village school teacher he had often asked for books, a regiment of guards or even a division. He no longer leaned on his stick but toyed with it as with a cane.

Elena's mother emerged from the dark corner and answered dryly: "Don't you know Sidorovich that we do not issue milk at the collective farm today?" "Sidorovich!" he repeated with a grimace and laughed affectedly, "Perhaps you've no water?"

The soldiers were still standing on the threshold, as it were, sniffing the room. From under his white eyebrows he cast a glance at Elena Pavlova and grinned showing his white teeth. Her mother brought a jug of water from the kitchen. Meanwhile Ivan Sidorovich thumbed over the books which lay on the table and threw them one by one on the floor. Mark saw his picture book go and bent down to pick it up. Ivan Sidorovich stepped on it with his foot and pushed the boy back with his stick. Mark scowled and cried furiously, "We'll get right out of here but you and Hitler are dogs." Ivan Sidorovich looked at him with a heavy, leaden, expression and raised his stick silently to hit the boy on the head but Elena Pavlova managed to avert the blow and cried. "Comrade how brave you are!" "I am not your comrade. At eight o'clock this evening you will be at the club, you will take in two officers. We know that you will make up your mind to remain non-partisan," he smiled evilly. He turned on his heels and walked out.

The soldiers again talked among themselves and cast their eyes around the room. An embroidered handbag hung on the wall. With a foolish grin the white eyebrowed soldier took it from the wall and thrust it inside his coat. Another soldier appropriated a watch lying on the bureau. A third kicking the teacher to one side with boots covered with mud began to rummage in the corner. Not finding anything and seeing that his comrades were leaving, he pulled the cloth from the table. The remaining books all fell to the floor with the writing set and a glass of water. A black puddle formed on the floor from the spilled ink. The soldier had behaved exactly as if no one else had been in the room. Standing in front of the mirror he twirled his mustache, winked at his reflection and seizing a little box of shells, hastened after the others.

Elena buried her head on the empty table. Her mother went over to her and looked over her shoulder which was still covered with the shawl. "That black soul with his tramps and his snake eyes spoke to you. He isn't our comrade. . . . Never mind, our people will come back. It won't be long and then we can live again."

Through the windows the tank creaked deafeningly, lifted its blunt muzzle and with a snort plunged forward.

There were also ecclesiastical Sidoroviches. The devious career of Polycarp Sikorskii terminated in his attempt to gain ascendancy by founding out of hand and under the benevolent eye of the German government an autocephalous Ukrainian Church of which he was to be the head. He appears to have mobilized a following from the remnant's of Petlura's party under whose short-lived government he had served in the ministry of education. As a quintessential Ukrainian he refused to speak Great Russian or to say Mass in Church Slavic. As late as 1940 he was in full schism. Through the mediation of another ambiguous figure, Metropolitan Dionysius of the Polish autocephalous Church, the German government agreed to register the new Ukrainian diocese. In reviewing the case, Patriarch Sergius, observed:

The role of Metropolitan Dionysius is not at all clear. Either he preferred the Ukrainian autocephalous Church to its Polish equivalent which was malingering under the protection of the Fascists or he was being polite to the schismatics, wishing to secure his own position in the Petluran Party. The autocephalous character of the Ukrainian Church is not supported by that Church itself, e.g., by any assembly or council of archpriests. . . . It is supported by the *Zemlyachestvo,* a kind of student or political club which does not even exist on Ukrainian territory but somewhere abroad, with the consent of the foreign German government which is now at war with the Ukraine.

Sikorskii was deposed by a council of Russian archbishops under the jurisdiction of Sergius, March 28, 1942.[9]

A similar hope of profiting by German favor was entertained by a group in the north under the leadership of Metropolitan Sergii Voskresenskii. In a pastoral addressed especially to the Orthodox of Lithuania, Latvia and Esthonia the Patriarch wrote:

In Riga in the beginning of August [1942] our Orthodox arch-priests, the vicars Jacob, archbishop of Yelgan, Paul bishop of Nerv, and Daniel Kovenskii, under the leadership of the Lithuanian metropolitan Sergii Voskresenskii who had no wish "to suffer affliction with the people of God" but preferred "to enjoy the pleasures of sin for a season," decided to do themselves well and nourish themselves with provisions from the Fascist table. Let others sacrifice themselves for their fatherland! Men's hair was standing on end at reading of the tortures inflicted by the Fascists on women, children and the wounded but Metropolitan Sergii Voskresenskii and his fellow "champions," the archbishops, tele-graphed Hitler that they were filled with admiration at the heroic struggle conducted [by Hitler] . . . and "prayed the Most High favorably to grant speedy and complete victory to the [Fascist] armies."

A council of bishops under Sergius (September 22, 1942) de-manded an immediate explanation of the conduct of these clerics to be sent both to the ecclesiastical authorities and to the public press. The decisions of the council were to be sent to newspapers abroad and Voskresenskii was deprived of his rectorship of the Church of the Transfiguration.[10]

Russian sentiment reacted to the German occupation in two characteristic ways. Among secular-minded Communists, to whom the materialist creed still seemed adequate, there was an

[9] *Russkaya Pravoslavnaya Tserkov i Velikaya Otechestvennaya Voina*, p. 22. Moscow, 1943.
[10] *Ibid.*, p. 35.

intensification of patriotism which expressed itself in feelings
and attitudes parallel in structure and tone with the feelings
and attitudes of religion. The attachment to the soil, the pride
in Russian independence, the intellectual and moral liberation
of the masses are all described in terms of the new ideology,
but the sense of the Russian land as inviolable and untouchable,
the consciousness of an historic destiny and an addiction to
broad culture are common elements in both the ancient and the
modern creeds. The extent to which Bolshevik faith was regarded as a creed is vividly illustrated by a Ukrainian story,
The Last Day of Dr. Onipko, by Natan Rybok[11] which describes first the disillusionment, then the self-discovery of a
doctor and gentleman of the old school during the German
invasion:

Dr. Onipko closed his eyes. It was dark in the room; only feeble
beams of light penetrated the blinds. He cleared his throat and
mechanically glanced in the mirror. A man in a gray jacket with
a white handkerchief emerging from the pocket looked back at
him from the round black frame. The face in the circle seemed to
him expressionless. The eyebrows were excessively shaggy. Horn-
rimmed glasses set on the nose and mustaches hung down over
somewhat protruding lips.

Dr. Onipko could no longer stand being the victim of uncertainty. What would be, would be; but in general he hoped for the
best. Whatever happens, always turns out for the best in the long
run. That is the way he had been reassuring his patients for the last
forty years. That is the way he tried to reassure himself. Having
made up his mind, he went to the window and tugged at the cord.
The heavy blinds parted and slid to the sides. Sunlight entered the
room.

He did not want to look at the street. It would be better that
way; again, not knowing why, he comforted himself. He seated
himself in his armchair and began to reflect. His eyes ran restlessly
to the walls and glass doors of the tall cupboards. The famous

[11] *Gnyevnoye Slovo,* p. 146. The English rendering is mine.

doctor's sharp eyes which at first glance had unerringly diagnosed the condition of his patients, were now directed to something else and were testing their penetration in another matter. The walls and cupboards did not disturb the flow of the doctor's thoughts.

"Nonetheless, I tried to do the right thing." His thoughts unrolled like a spool of thread. "Why should I become involved with the Germans a second time? In 1918 they treated me tactfully. I am no politician. I am a physician and yet. . . . At that time, in 1918 they did not disturb me. They issued specially a document protecting me. . . ."

Dr. Onipko took out a faded, folded paper. He opened it and read it through. How well-written! The style of the document pleased him. It ran thus. "The doctor is to be treated with respect, his property considered inviolable and in case of violation of this order, the guilty will be punished to the fullest extent of military law." Dr. Onipko returned the paper to his pocket. He sighed and appeared restless. Only day before yesterday his neighbor in the little square, the architect Terplinsky had startled him. "Leave," he had said, "sacrifice everything. You're making a great mistake to wait. It will be too late. You're a crank, you'll fall into the beast's mouth. It is utterly useless to stay."

This architect was a strange fellow. He had sacrificed everything, literally everything. In the depths of his soul, a conflict was going on in Dr. Onipko. But in the last analysis he was only a physician, not a politician. It would be as it had been in 1918. It was a good thing he had kept the document; it would come in useful. Everything would be all right. There would be changes but patients would begin coming again. Everything would be all right.

He got up and paced from room to room. He touched with his hands the glasses, the china, the candelabra on the grand piano. He looked in the cupboards and the sideboard and into the little room of his old servant Denis who had served him many years faithfully and well. Denis had also seen the Germans in 1918.

The doctor had asked Denis, "Is it all right for us to stay?" Denis had remained silent. He didn't even nod his head. Fear was in his eyes; his fingers stained with cigar smoke, trembled; he was silent. This meant that he disagreed. But Denis would not be sorry. Requests for treatment would come to the doctor; they would re-open the clinic; Denis would get his tips. Everything would be all right. Perhaps Denis was alarmed because his nephew was in the Red Army. But who would tell the Germans that?

Denis had been silent. There had been anguish in his eyes, in-describable anguish. That was bad. He had not needed any one else's anguish; he had enough of his own. Again he turned into the hallway. He pressed his ear against the door, then opened it and put his head out. The sign hung there and everything was as it should be, "Internist. Prof. I. J. Onipko. Office hours daily 2–5 P.M., except Sundays." He shut the door carefully and went into his office and relaxed. That was good, "except Sundays."

There was a prolonged ring and rattle at the door. Dr. Onipko sped like the wind out of the office. He paused in the front hall. The first thing that caught his weak rheumy eyes were Denis's gray mottled face and beyond there, no more, six men in tall caps, loaded revolvers in their hands. Single-headed silver eagles held the swastika in their beaks on the soldiers' sleeves and chests. The doctor's knees shook, betraying his alarm and his aching heart contracted. He did not say what he intended but repeated auto-matically:

"*Bitte, bitte,* how do you do?"

The tall officer shoved him aside with his elbow. Behind them they led in by the arm a man in German officer's dress. A bloody trail was left on the blue carpet. They laid the man on the couch.

"Doctor!" they called from the office.

He darted off. The officer who had shoved the doctor, looked him in the eye as if he were aiming a gun.

"Your papers."

Dr. Onipko hastily extended his cherished, well-preserved docu-ment. The officer glanced through it hastily, crushed it in his fist and flung it on the ground.

"A forgery!" he cried. "Bolshevik pieces. . . . Take care of the wounded man. *Schnell!*"

Dr. Onipko's hands shook. Nothing like this had ever happened to him. For the first time in his life he approached a patient with uncertain steps and his whole body ached with little, spasmodic shivers.

"*Schnell*, I said. Or are you deaf?" The officer raised his hand.

The doctor bent over his patient. He saw immediately that a surgeon was needed. He turned to the officer.

"I am an internist," he said, trying to regain his composure. "You must call a surgeon."

"You're a Bolshevik knave. You refuse to attend a German officer."

Dr. Onipko tried to explain. He was a physician, only a physician. He was neutral. Politics were not his sphere. But the officer refused to listen and shook his fist before his face and screamed as if to a deaf man.

"You have refused aid to a German officer. All right. Arrest him!"

The soldiers took him by the arms and pushed him out the door. He had already heard from there the sound of crockery and a huge crash. Before the house was a little group of people. The soldier pushed Onipko into their ranks with the butt of his rifle. They were surrounded by soldiers, the doctor lost his glasses. Screwing up his eyes he looked around helplessly. Someone stopped and picked up his glasses. "Such a respectable old man, with a rifle-butt!" A woman's voice whispered sympathetically. Strange, confusing thoughts assailed the doctor. Everything seemed to have been stood on its head in a single day. Another world had arisen within the walls of that house. On the third story, his own windows; he knew them perfectly. The third one had a swinging pane and the wind was moving it. How many times had he tried to remind Denis to send for the locksmith and repair the bolt. He was being herded with the women and children along the street toward Kreschatik but he continued to think about the bolt. It served him as a moral support. He marched in single file with the women, seized with an inexplicable indifference. Only his heart pained dreadfully and actually he felt very unwell. He asked Denis whether he had the key to the garage. Unobserved by the guard Denis slipped the key in his palm and he clenched it. The feel of the cold steel seemed to calm him.

He went on without looking back. He did not notice that the crowd behind him was growing. The soldiers were turning everyone out of the houses. Along the Kreschatik they passed through ranks of soldiers. In the middle of the street tanks stood ready for action. The barrels of guns and the muzzles of rifles pointed threateningly at the windows of the silent houses.

When the crowd of women, children, and old men in which the doctor was lost were driven into the broad courtyard enclosed by a high fence, he awoke from his reverie. The day had flung in his face handfuls of fear and dread. Drawing his head erect, bareheaded, hot and exhausted as he was (he had not walked so far for a long time), Dr. Onipko stood trying to think through this lightning transition from the past to the present. It was as if a stone wall lay on his old shoulders. He was alone, absolutely alone. There was no one to put in a word for him, no one to lift a finger. He was alone. Everything that he had left back there on Malo Zhitorsky seemed beside the point, except that Denis was here. He couldn't quite look Denis in the face.

"Just as in 1918," this notion too was extinguished. Of all the joyful past there remained pressed hard in his palm, the key to the garage where his machine stood, the present of the city soviet on the day of his anniversary celebration.

The anniversary. . . ! The auditorium of the Franko Theater rose in his memory, the blaze of lights, the ovations, the flowers, the congratulations.

Immersed in his own thoughts, he had not heard the officers call one after the other from the crowd for questioning. When they came to him and led him off for questioning, he still had heard nothing, wrapped as he was in his own grief. He emerged from his own distress as if he had stepped over a threshold startled by the harsh shout of the officer.

In the first instant he managed to see a horrible piece of ruthlessness: a little child transfixed by a bayonet, its mother's hands stretched pleadingly toward its murderer. . . .

When the officer impatiently demanded his papers, Dr. Onipko preserved silence. They shot above his ear and he heard someone groan and recognized Denis's voice.

"You refuse to answer?" the officer asked in a terrible voice, coming nearer and pressing his revolver against Onipko's breast.

"Are you a Bolshevik?"

Dr. Onipko looked around involuntarily, as if he was looking for what was called "bolshevik." He cast a glance at Denis and all the rest. He saw in the eyes of each one of them a firmness, an invincible faith and a stubborn gleam. Then holding his head high, he looked straight into the officer's blood-shot eyes and pronounced gravely, as if it were an oath:

"I am a Bolshevik."

Immediately a shot rang out. Guns roared over the Dnieper. The aerial bombs rent the land beyond the Dnieper. The streets of Old Kiev ran in turbulent streams down to the Dnieper laden with the irresistible force of a great sorrow. But Dr. Onipko lay in the muddy courtyard. His heart was pierced with a German bullet but his face was serene and peaceful as if in the last moment of life he had come to understand the truth about human existence.

The reaction to the German occupation among religious people was no less intense and no less characteristic. The psychological change from what had gone before was in fact less abrupt and less striking. The Church had survived vigorous persecution for more than twenty years. When the worst enemies of religion ceased to be the representatives of their own government and became the hostile and intrusive Germans, the result was a relaxation of the tension between the two equally Russian forces and the formation of a common front against a common foe. The temper of Orthodoxy became patriotic and the savage determination of all Russians to defend the fatherland and all it signified from desecration tended to reach beyond the ideology of the moment to deeper psychological reserves and defenses.

On the outbreak of the war Sergius issued a pastoral to all

the faithful in Russia. It is a classic formulation of the new Orthodox patriotism, breaks cleanly with the patient watchfulness of revolutionary years and asserts as natural and inevitable the right of Russian Orthodoxy to contribute in its own way and on the terms of its own faith to the national effort.

It is not the first time that the Russian people have had to endure such trials. With God's help and in his good time, it will scatter the hostile Fascist forces like ashes. Our ancestors did not lose heart even under the most adverse circumstances, because they were mindful not of personal danger and concerns but of their sacred duty to their country and faith, and they emerged victorious. We shall not sully their glorious name and we, Orthodox, are their kindred in flesh and in faith. Our homeland will be protected by arms and by every national means, by a complete readiness to serve our country in this terrible hour of trial in the way each one is able. There is work for laborers, farmers, scientists, women and men, young and old. Everyone must take on his share of work, of care and of skill in the common enterprise. . . . Our Orthodox Church has always shared the nation's destiny. With it she has undergone trials and taken comfort in its successes. She will not abandon her country on this occasion. . . . It is for us to be especially mindful of Christ's command, "Greater love has no one than he who lays down his life for his friends." Not only he who dies on the field of battle lays down his life for his country and its well-being but also everyone who sacrifices himself, his health or personal advantage, for the nation. At such a time, when our country is mobilizing everyone for the task, it is not enough for us, the pastors of the church, merely to look silently on what goes on about us, to encourage the timid, to comfort the distressed, to recall the hesitant to duty and God's will. But if, in addition to this, the silence of the pastor indicates his carelessness of the flock and by subtle reasoning counts the possible gains from abroad, that will be direct treason to his country and to his pastoral obligation, in proportion to the Church's need of pastors, who really bear their responsibility "for Jesus' sake and not for a morsel of bread," as S. Demetrius of Rostov expresses it. Let us lay down our own lives with those of our flock. Countless thousands of our Orthodox soldiers have trod the way of sacrifice and have laid down their lives for the nation and the faith at all times of hostile invasion of our nation. They died heedless of glory. Considering only the fact that the nation had need of their sacrifices, they made that sacrifice in every way that they could, even with their lives. The Church of Christ gives its blessing to all the Orthodox for the protection of the sacred boundaries of our nation. God grant us victory.

The leaders of Orthodoxy were, however, not content with feelings and words but translated both into action. It must not be forgotten that in so far as the atheistic compaign failed, the soldiers who were not its converts remained loyal to their religion. When Nikolai, metropolitan and exarch of the entire Ukraine was compelled to leave his see at Lutzk, he did not retire from the combat zone but ministered tirelessly to soldiers and civilians along the front. His services were so needed and so appreciated that he was appointed by Sergii metropolitan of Kiev and Galicia and exarch of the entire Ukraine.

Sergius and his clergy did not lose sight of the opportunity given by the war of demonstrating their willingness to sacrifice themselves for the nation and thus offset the bad impression created in part by darkened counsel, in part by hostile propaganda in the years of famine. Millions of rubles poured into the funds for national defense. A tank corps bearing the name of Dmitri Donskoi was financed by the offerings of the faithful on the initiative of Sergius and his clergy. In a charge to his people the metropolitan of Leningrad Alexei, now patriarch, wrote:

The message of Metropolitan Sergii to the pastors and flocks of the Russian Church summoned all the faithful in this terrible hour of danger which envelops our fatherland, to a united defense of our great country, every man to the full measure of his strength. In this message it was said in the name of the Church that it, Holy Church, "blesses with a heavenly blessing this common enterprise."

And this voice of the first arch-pastor of the Russian Church proved to be no "voice crying in the wilderness." All the faithful responded to this appeal. All united without differences at the moment of the common peril, as citizens of one great Union in one effort to determine how each one might help share in the common task of defending the fatherland. Upon this undertaking blessed by the Church, not only youths not yet called to military service but men past their prime and even old men enlisted as volunteers at the front, fully prepared even to lay down their lives for the integrity, honor and welfare of their beloved country.

Te Deums in the churches and petitions for a Russian victory found an echo in the heart of every worshipper. These now have but one thought, one prayer, "God grant that we may conquer the bloodthirsty and wicked enemy, crush Fascism which has brought misery and destruction upon all mankind and may He restore us all to cheerful living and to happy productive work."

Wishes have been expressed on the part of the faithful of various churches that the considerable amounts deposited in the churches, in some very considerable, as much as 100,000 rubles, be given to the government for the defense fund for war needs. Various small sums contributed by the faithful were also diverted to these needs.

The following incident occurred recently in a church in Leningrad. Some unknown pilgrims brought in a package and placed it before the icon of St. Nicholas. In the package were nearly one hundred and fifty gold ten ruble coins of pre-revolutionary money. They were immediately deposited in the bank for defense needs.

Does not all this show that the sentiment of love for the mother-country has been roused in everyone and that the terrible danger which Fascism has brought with it has been sensed by all, so that they have directed all their forces to one goal, that of saving the country at whatever cost?

The Russian people saw and knew from the example of Germany enslaved by Fascism, and from other countries unwillingly betrayed, to what a pass their Fascism has brought them. They perceived that Fascism was the ruin of everything which had been won by centuries of effort by humanity as a whole, of everything cheerful and productive. And now it sees plainly and senses the whole horror which the merciless enemy brings with him, falling treacherously on our land and attempting to overthrow and destroy the gains we have made by hard work.

Actually there has fallen on us what the Psalmist describes as "the iniquity of the proud," which could not look quietly on the acquired riches of our country and judging us by themselves, were unwilling to believe in our righteousness. Their suspicion and hatred of us caused them to embark upon a course ultimately destructive to themselves; by arms and bloodshed, they have attempted to enslave and subject us.

It is needless to say much about the barbarism with which the enemy operates and which everyone can see. It is unnecessary to dwell upon that purely Teutonic *Schrechlichkeit* with which it tries by every means to intimidate its victims. Many clergy and laity who have escaped the terrors of Fascism have spoken on this subject. These living witnesses relate how Hitler organizes the destruction of women, children and the aged in occupied districts, kills off the severely wounded, bombs hospitals and trains full of peaceful citizens, and dwelling houses. All this is a peculiar form of psychological warfare, an inhuman bestial kind of conflict.

He has fallen on us with special fury, for he particularly hates us not only as Slavs but as representatives of a form of culture and progress eradicated by the Fascists in every sphere. And he covers all this beastliness and horror by the false and blasphemous formula, "Christian Progress," disregarding the fact that by the frightful destruction of everything held dear by the peoples who are already his slaves in both the material and spiritual spheres, he has long shown the world that in Fascism there is nothing holy, no ideals of any kind except universal deceit and enslavement.

From its attitude to the Church, to Orthodoxy (in Yugoslavia), to Catholicism, to the representatives of all conquered and enslaved countries, it is possible to judge what would be its policy toward the Orthodox Church, in view of the special hatred it has for our country. It would mean the Church's total extinction, just because it has enjoyed complete freedom not only theoretically, in accordance with our Soviet law, but also in fact.

It is no novelty in history that madmen should arise with dreams of conquering the whole world. The "Roman Peace" as Roman imperialism called itself, in the course of centuries attempted to realize this proud vision. It had on its side technical skill, force, power, education, superiority in numbers, cruelty, pillage, enslavement. Everything was converted into weapons for conquering the world. But how did this dream end? The world was not conquered but the *Pax Romana* crumbled to dust. It is no novelty to our native land to be attacked by a foe dreaming of conquering us. Napoleon dreamed of it and seemed close to his goal in tearing out the heart of Russia, Moscow. But precisely at this point he was destined not to find victory but defeat and decisive defeat, for the whole nation rose up against the enemy. So it is now. The whole nation and its victory is assured. It is assured by the common will to victory, the unflinching courage of the troops with their complete contempt for death and willingness to lay down their lives for their country, by an unswerving faith in the triumphant power of a righteous cause.

War is a terrible and devastating thing for anyone who undertakes it needlessly, unjustly, in the expectation of plunder and the enslavement of others. Upon such falls contempt and the wrath of heaven for the blood and suffering they have caused their own and other people.

But war is a holy thing for those who undertake it of necessity, in defense of their rights and of their native land. In taking up arms in such a cause they are crusaders for the right and when they are wounded and suffer and lay down their lives for their kin and country, they follow in the martyrs' footsteps to an imperishable and immortal crown. Therefore the Church also blesses these undertakings and everything which every Russian does in defense of his country.

The undoubted successes of our troops, acknowledged by the enemy themselves, against a powerful but already weakening foe speaks for the fact that our faith in victory is not vain. The immutable law that he who unjustly draws the sword will perish by the sword actually suspends a sword of Damocles over the criminal head of Fascism and the time is at hand when this sword of punishment will let the whole weight of its inevitable fate fall upon the enemy and will crush it.

The Church calls aloud for the defense of the mother-country. Filled with faith in God's help in a righteous cause, it prays for the full and final victory over the enemy.

In *The Truth about Religion in Russia* facsimiles of the checks for the contributions made by the Church are published and in the companion volume of documents the telegrams exchanged between the patriarch and Stalin are reproduced. It is obvious to anyone sensitive to diplomatic usage that the form and tone of the telegrams exchanged between Sergius and Alexei and Stalin suggest circumspection and certain reserves on both sides. Where national interest was involved, however, those reserves were cast aside and behind the formal phrases of recognition of Stalin as chief of the state and supreme commander of the armed forces lies the conviction that the safety and welfare not only of Soviet territory but of Holy Russia are being guarded by the state. It is important to emphasize the similarity between the *carmen saeculare* of Horace and the mood of these effusions. The security offered by the state is a real security and the emotional reaction to it is sincere and unequivocal. It is significant that broader commitments are avoided on both sides. It is, however, equally clear that an institution which has survived the brutal persecution meted out to it by the Bolsheviks in the past twenty-five years and which was still prepared not only to pray for its persecutors but to contribute 6,000,000 rubles to the maintenance of its armed forces cannot be a negligible factor in the policy of a stable and forward-looking government. There are deep forces at work here and it is clear that their combination could go far in the direction of genuine religious freedom within the structure of a socialist state. The recent trend of government action in Church affairs and its more conservative and less tentative ethical position on such fundamental issues as marriage and the family point hopefully in this direction.

With the attack of Germany on Russia came Winston Churchill's historic declaration of solidarity between all enemies of the Reich and a radical change in policy toward Russia by the Allies with England in the lead. Churchill, Roosevelt, and Stalin saw clearly that concerted military action would not suffice in the long run without some reconciliation of ideological differences. American and British public opinion were affected not only by the economic policies of the Soviet Union but by the social and personal ideals encouraged by it. The former produced panic, the latter resentment. The attack on religion had been regarded not only as a campaign against the Church but as a frontal assault upon the foundations of long-established personal and social standards. The tentative attitude toward the family as an institution and the discrediting of traditional sexual barriers had convinced conservative elements in Britain and America that not only economic but moral chaos threatened the world. This threat, it was felt, was implicit in the Communist program of the liberation of the working classes everywhere from the yoke of autocratic and bourgeois politics and their protection against the ideological weapons of religion and middle class morality. The fluctuation of public sentiment toward Russia had its repercussions in the ecclesiastical sphere. The two churches outside Russia most deeply concerned with Orthodoxy were the Anglican and the Roman Catholic. Both were animated by genuine religious concern but each had political interests and these took widely different forms.

Anglican interest in the Russian Church is of long standing. At the time of the Reformation there was more interest in Russian Orthodoxy which increased when trade relations between the two countries became more active and Englishmen went to Russia to look after English business interests there. It will be remembered that Peter the Great visited Lambeth Palace and conversed on theological matters with some English bishops. It is not impossible that his own ecclesiastical reforms were influenced by his observation of the Established Church. A sustained and practical interest in the Russian Church and a desire to seek union with her on terms of reasonable compromise was, however, the product of a later age and of the genius of Newman. In his *Via Media* Newman conceived the Universal Church as living three separate existences in the Roman, Eastern Orthodox, and Anglican communions. Years later (1882) he epitomized this view in his preface to William Palmer's *Notes of a Visit to the Russian Church* and described Palmer as

one of those earnest-minded and devout men, forty years since, who, deeply convinced of the great truth that our Lord had instituted, and still acknowledges and protects, a visible Church—one, individual, and integral—Catholic, as spread over the earth, Apostolic as co-eval with the Apostles of Christ, and Holy, as being the dispenser of His Word and Sacraments—considered it at present to exist in three main branches, or rather in a triple presence, the Latin, the Greek, and the Anglican, these three being one and the same Church, distinguishable from each other only by secondary, fortuitous, and local, though important, characteristics. And, whereas the whole Church in its fulness was, as they believed, at once and severally Anglican, Greek, and Latin, so in turn each one of those three was the whole Church; whence it followed that, whenever any one of the three was present, the other two, by the nature of the case, were absent, and therefore the three could not have direct relations with each other, as if they were three substantive bodies, there being no real difference between them except the external accident of place. Moreover since, as has been said, on a given territory, there could not be more than one of the three, it followed that Christians generally, wherever they were, were bound to recognize, and had a claim to be recognized by that one, ceasing to belong to the Anglican Church, as Anglican, when they were at Rome, and ignoring Rome as Rome, when they found them-

selves at Moscow. Lastly, not to acknowledge this inevitable outcome of the initial idea of the Church, viz., that it was both everywhere and one, was bad logic, and to act in opposition to it was
nothing short of setting up altar against altar, that is, the hideous
sin of schism, and a sacrilege.

This I conceive to be the formal teaching of Anglicanism; this
is what we held and professed in Oxford forty years ago.

In the early stages of the Oxford Movement, none of the
original group was led to map out in detail the relations between Eastern Orthodoxy and Anglicanism, much less to ex-
plore in practice their common ground. This prospect, however, fired the imagination of William Palmer, a young deacon
and fellow of Magdalen, who proceeded to devote to this task
a zeal and enthusiasm equal to that expended by other Anglo-
Catholics of his day on what seemed to be the more pressing
question of reunion with Rome. Mr. Palmer confided his hopes
to the President of Magdalen, Dr. Routh, and prepared under
his critical eye a scorchingly censored memorandum which was
presented to the Grand Duke Alexander on his visit to Oxford
in 1893. The substance and form of the petition were as quaint
as its authorship and revision would lead one to expect. It proposed that "some Russian ecclesiastic, capable of examining the
theology of our churches," be sent to Oxford, to reside at Magdalen, learn English from Mr. Palmer himself and study Anglican theology, "that so through him the contents of some of
our best books may be made known to His Imperial Majesty
and to the Bishops of the Eastern Communion." Mr. Palmer in
turn proposed to go to Russia to undertake a like course in
Orthodox theology and ceremonial under the patronage of the
tsar. The object of these visits was to promote "the reunion of
the two communions, separated only by misunderstandings and
want of intercourse." In the original draft the petition ended
with the amazing peroration: "May God bless the throne of
the Emperor of Russia, and may all the peoples committed to

him obey him as a father. May he never see the anarchical principles of heretical Protestantism coming to disturb his empire and its churches; and may it be given to him, on the occurrence of some just opportunity, to deliver the East from the yoke of the Infidels." The last sentence was deleted by Dr. Routh. "The first clause," the President observed, "will not be understood, and the second will seem un-English."

The Grand Duke graciously accepted the petition but Mr. Palmer's prospective Russian pupil never arrived. Nothing daunted, he resolved to carry out his share of the bargain and armed with credentials from the British ambassador and a letter of introduction from Dr. Routh to which the Fellows of Magdalen flatly declined to subscribe, Mr. Palmer set forth for Russia in August, 1840. If Palmer's petition to Alexander had been quaint, Dr. Routh's communication written in the most pontifical style was a veritable museum piece. It contained the startling injunction:

Further, I ask, and even adjure in the name of Christ, all the most holy Archbishops and Bishops, and especially the Synod itself, that they will examine him as to the orthodoxy of his faith with a charitable mind, and, if they find in him all that is necessary to the integrity of the true and saving faith, then that they will also admit him to communion in the Sacraments. I would have him submit and conform himself in all things to the injunctions and admonitions of the Russian bishops, and neither affirming anything nor doing anything, contrary to the faith and doctrine of the British Churches.

In an unguarded moment Dr. Howley, the Archbishop of Canterbury, declared his readiness to countersign Dr. Routh's letter, but having examined the text sent word by his chaplain that he did not feel able to put his name to any such document.

Lord Clanricarde's letters, however, proved most useful and Mr. Palmer's visit was full of interest. He met Count Protasov, the High Procurator of the Holy Synod, the Church historian Mouraviev, and a number of Russian ecclesiastics. There were long and fascinating theological discussions, delightful trips to monasteries and churches with memorable services and pleasant encounters. Palmer's obvious sincerity, personal charm, and remarkable familiarity with Russian theology and practice impressed his new friends but his main purpose in coming to Russia left them confused and unconvinced. To the suggestion that he be admitted forthwith to communion Count Protasov remarked, *"C'est fort,"* and the Metropolitan of Moscow, Philaret, politely but firmly refused his formal request. Mr. Palmer sadly recorded the event:

I received from Mr. Mouraviev the written answer of the Metropolitan of Moscow to my letter. It was to this effect; that he who would receive the communion from a diocesan bishop, must submit absolutely and without restriction to all the doctrine, discipline and ritual of the Orthodox (Eastern) Church. But to make union or reconciliation with any concession or allowance, however small, is beyond the power of a diocesan bishop, and can be done only by Synods. At the same time he returned to me a Latin copy of the XXXIX Articles, with the corner of the leaves carefully turned down at Articles XIX, XXI, and XXII.

Mouraviev attempted to soften the blow. In a farewell interview he said:

The impression you have made upon the Metropolitan and upon all of us is most favorable to your Church. We have all had the greatest pleasure in conversing with you, and I must say, though you are only a deacon, yet the cause of your Church could not have been better represented. . . . With respect to the communion, though as things are there are obstacles to our giving it to you, I hope the time may come when it may be otherwise; meanwhile we must on both sides content ourselves with the consciousness that there is a unity of spirit between us, and a desire, ours not less than yours, of a visible and formal union.

I have dealt with Palmer's mission at such length because it is typical of so many attempts at *rapprochement* between the Anglican and Russian Churches since that time. Great amiability, sound Christian feeling, and personal good will have characterized the attitudes of both sides, but an inability to surmount the prejudices and control the instincts of ecclesiastical provincialism have blocked the way. In a conversation with Fr. Maloff, Palmer urged the necessity of ultimate reunion with Rome and was answered, "Ah, you will never bring our bishops and archimandrites to that, for they regard the Church as confined to the East." In discussing a petition for reunion between the Anglican and Russian Churches in 1851, James Mason Neale wrote to his friend Webb, "I don't see much to object to in the form of the petition except that it should state more plainly what we want. No one could say whether we are asking them to consecrate us Bishops, or receive us to communion without Bishops. . . . But I think the letter might be much better done. It is so English."

In 1888 on the occasion of a religious festival at Kiev, Archbishop Benson sent greetings to the metropolitan of that see and to his surprise received a reply asking on what specific terms the archbishop's amiable aspirations toward reunion could be effected. A statement was drawn up, suggesting intercommunion, the recognition of the validity of Anglican orders, and an exchange of views on differences of doctrine and discipline. The matter was dropped.

In 1896 Lord Halifax persuaded Queen Victoria of the suitability of sending an episcopal representative to the coronation of Nicholas II. Archbishop Benson agreed and the learned Bishop Creighton was chosen and dispatched with the greetings of the archbishop. He dined with the emperor, preached twice at the English Church and on his return sent a description of the coronation to the queen. Victoria replied, "The Queen is most grateful to the Bishop of Peterborough for his

enlarged and beautiful account of the Coronation at Moscow.
. . . How the Queen wishes she could have seen it."

In 1897 Archbishop Maclagan decided to visit Moscow. He
was accompanied by Mr. Birkbeck and had originally planned
to take his wife with him, but this prospect so horrified his advisers that "the Lady Archbishop of York," as she was called
by a well-meaning Russian correspondent, remained at home.
There was the usual round of festivities: an audience with the
tsar, sermons in the English Church and visits to Russian services at which on one occasion a place was reserved for the archbishop in the choir.

During most of the nineteenth century the movement for
reunion depended on the initiative of gifted and earnest individuals: William Palmer, George Williams, James Neale, William Birkbeck, and Athelston Riley. As Anglo-Catholicism
grew and acquired substance and organization, groups arose
to foster mutual understanding and friendship with Orthodoxy. From the English Church Union, the Eastern Church
Association, later called the Anglican and Eastern Association,
emerged and established "practical measures for increasing understanding through visiting lecturers and a wisely planned
series of meetings and publications in the English language."
More recently the Fellowship of SS. Alban and Sergius under
Fr. Brandreth, O.G.S. and here in America the Orthodox and
Anglican Fellowship "have helped greatly in spreading understanding between Russian Orthodox and Western Christians,
particularly among students and lay people."[12] The Ecumenical Movement with its conferences at Oxford and Edinburgh
have been helpful in this regard and perhaps even more the
informal gatherings and discussions at High Leigh attended
by distinguished theologians of the Russian seminary in Paris.

Mr. Palmer's visit resulted in a long correspondence with

[12] Paul B. Anderson, *People, Church and State in Modern Russia* (New
York: The Macmillan Company, 1944), p. 5.

the Slavophile and lay theologian Khomiakov. Neither side was convinced by the arguments of the other and Khomiakov seems to have been driven further from the English Church than ever, but important questions were ventilated and unexpected points of agreement and disagreement were discovered. James Neale's historical scholarship roused not only respect but enthusiasm for his work on the Eastern Church. The appearances of English ecclesiastics at Russian court and Church functions stimulated interest and good will. Liddon visited Russia in 1867 and wrote:

Today I feel that, for the first time in my life, I stand face to face with the Eastern Church. . . . Right or wrong, it is a vast, energetic and most powerful body, with an evident hold upon the heart of the largest of European empires, indeed a force within the limits of Russia to which I believe there is no parallel in the West. . . .

Some gestures were made from the Russian side of which perhaps the most moving was the presence of Fr. Popov, chaplain to the Russian Embassy, and the Archimandrite Stratuli at the dedication of St. Margaret's Convent in 1865 as a tribute to the work of the bitterly persecuted Father Founder, J. M. Neale. Before the last war, however, there were not many opportunities for Russian clergy to appear in English churches and difficult questions of discretion and etiquette were seldom raised. The situation after the war and especially after the Bolshevik Revolution was quite different. Russian emigrants fleeing the Revolution and securing a precarious foothold abroad were divided into numerous factions, and these in turn received varying degrees of support from older *émigrés* and from Anglican and other organizations. The parties of Tikhon, Vvedenskii, and Antonin in Russia and the unhappy Karlowitz Synod which did such poor service to the Church at home, complicated the picture and distorted perspectives. Political and religious principles and attachments were not clearly distinguished. Violent feeling and precipitate action prevailed over sound judgment and circumspection. The emigrants needed money badly and sometimes showed their appreciation for help or anticipated favors by making ecclesiastical concessions for which no adequate authority could be adduced or permanence assured. Isolated acts of intercommunion were reported. Anglican churches were generously offered and gratefully accepted for Russian services. The theological principle of *oikonomia* was stretched to permit a lively appreciation of approximations to Orthodox dogma and strivings toward it. With such encouragement the Anglican policy of reunion became more aggressive.

In spite of a growing and increasingly effective enthusiasm among Anglo-Catholics for reunion with the Russian Church, no fundamental concessions to Anglican claims have been made by competent authority and little eagerness felt outside Anglo-Catholic circles for closer association between the two communions. The reasons for this are clear and can be precisely stated:

1. From the Russian point of view the Anglican Church is a schism from a schism. This break can be repaired only by a return to Roman allegiance on the part of the English Church followed by a return of Western Christendom to Orthodoxy, or by a direct submission by the Anglican Church to Orthodox obedience.

2. From the Russian point of view also, the Anglican Church was bred in heresy, has openly proclaimed heresy in its official pronouncements, the XXXIX Articles, and has no convincing doctrinal unity on points regarded as fundamental to saving faith by Russian theologians.

3. The drive toward reunion with Russian Orthodoxy has not issued from a united conviction of the need for such a step among Anglicans, but has been used both to offset the merci-

less snub given to Anglican orders by Roman theologians, especially since Leo XIII's inquiry, and as a gambit in the controversy between Anglo-Catholics and Anglicans with other views on the nature of orders in the Anglican communion and the meaning of the whole sacramental system. Neither of those questions affected the Russians, but they were not slow to see their bearing not only on the situation in the Anglican Church but on any working arrangement between that Church and themselves.

In comparing the policies of the Anglican and Roman Churches toward Russian Orthodoxy certain broad distinctions must be made clear. Unlike the Church of England, the Roman Church has long occupied a secure position on Russian soil. In the territory politically fluctuating between Poland and Russia it has had control over large masses of population and its right to this control was, as we have seen, confirmed and strengthened by Peter I and Catherine II. Furthermore the policy of the Vatican in Russia has always been aggressive and the hope of large successes through conversion or negotiation or both has never been abandoned. It is not surprising that in spite of the law against proselytism and numerous repressive measures, Roman propaganda had its effect and between 1905-9 it was estimated that 233,000 persons had abjured Orthodoxy and submitted to Rome. Russians on their part have always resented Catholics as intruders and kept glowingly alive the theological animus engendered by the Photian schism and the Council of Florence.

At the close of World War I the Roman Church has been estimated at 8,000,000 in Russia. The collapse during the revolutionary years was spectacular and devastating. The Bolsheviks were no less hostile to Rome than to Orthodoxy and Catholic dioceses and parishes suffered the same disabilities and persecutions as did the Orthodox. They were despoiled of land, churches, plate, and other precious objects. Their educational institutions were closed and religious instruction, except for sermons, forbidden. In addition to this they were vulnerable to attack by the Orthodox clergy who at times took advantage of revolutionary conditions to discredit and weaken their rivals.

At the time of the famine the Pope sent a special mission of relief to Russia primarily to feed starving children. It was headed by an American Jesuit, Fr. Walsh, who overcame the almost insuperable difficulties put in his path by the Soviet authorities and administered the material and sums put at his disposal with skill and effect. A convincing and moving account of this mission has been published by Msgr. d'Herbigny. A bald but impressive statement of its work is given by Fisher in his report of the A.R.A.:

The National Catholic Welfare Council was one of the original members of the European Relief Council, but did not establish its own organization in Russia, affiliated with the A.R.A., until March, 1922. An appeal from the Vatican for funds for Russian relief received such a generous response that the Catholic Mission was able to carry out a mass feeding program which reached 157,507 persons in the districts of Crimea, Orenburg, Moscow, Rostov, Don, and Krasnodar. In addition to this feeding, which was conducted without distinction as to race, religion, or politics, the Mission imported and distributed $250,000 worth of textiles and medicines. Although the funds supporting the Catholic program came from Europe as well as America, the food purchases, amounting to about $750,000, were all made in America by the A.R.A. in behalf of the National Catholic Welfare Council. $20,000 in food packages were distributed to individuals by the Mission. The Catholics signed a separate agreement with the Soviet Government for the continuation of their work after July 1923.[13]

In spite of its beneficent effect Moscow was not favorable to the Vatican relief mission. As in the case of Orthodox funds

[13] H. H. Fisher, *The Famine in Soviet Russia 1919–23* (Hoover War Library Publications, No. 9, 1927).

raised abroad, it drew too marked attention to the solicitude and effectiveness of institutions which it was the wish of the Communist party to discredit. In the following year, therefore, when Archbishop Cieplak of Leningrad refused to obey the laws relating to confiscation of Church property and the cessation of religious instruction and threatened his clergy with excommunication if they followed the government's instructions, he was promptly arrested with seventeen of his clergy and after trials, the grim details of which have been vividly described by Captain MacCullach, was sentenced to death. The sentence was later commuted to imprisonment but his colleague, Msgr. Budkievicz, was executed and the others sentenced to from three to ten years imprisonment.

To judge these trials in their true perspective it must be remembered that the fundamental issue involved was not a religious one but the integrity of the Soviet Constitution and the right of the new government to define and enforce its own conception of civil obligations and criminal liability. There can be no question that the Catholic hierarchy proposed to force the government to yield on points involving differences between Catholic and Communist principle. In appealing from specific government legislation on the title of Church property and the control of education to the broad principle of freedom of conscience, Cieplak chose ground which he could not defend. The provocation offered to the government was identical with that offered by the Patriarch Tikhon and the trials of the two men ran parallel courses. The state was determined to assert and act on its own sovereign rights, and the protests from abroad against the inhumanity of the trials only confirmed the authorities in their determination to show that they meant business and that the new order was not to be trifled with or altered by appeals to consideration which the state did not recognize as valid.

This larger issue of principle was intensified by the attitude of the Vatican toward the Revolution and the Bolshevik state in general. The fact cannot be ignored that in spite of its international and supranational character, the Roman Church is a political force and has consistently opposed the rise and spread of Communism. The reaction of the Papacy to religious persecutions in Russia has been much more immediate and much less guarded than in the case of similar persecutions in Germany or even Italy. The unequivocal support given by the Church to Franco and its facile compromises with Mussolini have indicated that Roman Catholic polemic against Communism would be backed by every weapon at the Pope's disposition.

When the Constitution was changed in 1929 to prohibit religious propaganda Pope Pius XII made a striking gesture of protest and appointed March 19 (St. Joseph's Day) as a day of the worldwide intercession for Russia. The Holy Father offered a Mass with special intention at the Tomb of St. Peter and issued an encyclical.

The policy of the Vatican toward Russia since the Revolution has been animated in part by its sense of international guardianship of religious interests, in part by its concern for the large Catholic population in Russia and Poland. Undoubtedly in the minds of some the possibility has presented itself of ambitious missionary enterprise which might regain for the Roman Church ground which Orthodoxy had lost. This possibility has been sounded out on more than one occasion and papal emissaries have visited Russia for that purpose. It has even been advanced as a practical program by outsiders. Since the outbreak of the war Stalin has on occasions given smiling if inscrutable encouragement to such proposals. The impression made abroad might be favorable and he knows his people well enough to be sure of their immunity to Roman fever.

Chapter VI

PROSPECTS

M ANY CRITICS OF MODERN POLITICAL THE-
ory have noted the similarity between Russian Communism
and religion. Keynes wrote in his *Persuasive Essays* that "if
Communism achieves a certain success, it will achieve it, not
as an improved economic technique, but as a religion." Laski
has said:

Communism interests the new generation because, alone among
the welter of competing gospels, it has known how to win sacrifice
from its devotees in the name of a great ideal. It offers the prospect
the clue to the success of all great religions—of losing one's life in
order to find it. There is poverty, there is intellectual error, there is
grave moral wrong; but there is also unlimited hope. These have
been characteristic of all great religious movements. They do not
seem to disturb their power eventually to triumph.[1]

This analogy, like all analogies between emotionally charged
and appealing social and political systems and religion must be
drawn with caution. There are significant pluses and minuses
on both sides of the equation that do not cancel out and constitute exceptions that test and limit the application of the rule.
The truth is that social and political, as well as religious, ideals
involve responses which are relatively uniform in their psychological structure. Human nature, thus roused, tends to treat its

[1] "Position of Communism," *Foreign Affairs* XI, October, 1932, p. 105.

environment in similar ways and to attach the same significance to the objects of its interests, however differently these objects may be conceived and their selection from the range of human experience determined. Objects of attachment and veneration of love and dependence and of hostility and aggression appear in all comprehensive views of life, though these objects may be very differently located in the environment and variously described in the language of theology, philosophy, sociology, and politics.

The theory of Russian Communism, as we have seen, is the social philosophy of Marx and Engels which made significant contact with Russian thought in the 1880's and 1890's and extended its influence rapidly among radical and revolutionary groups up to its victorious emergence as the official ideology of the new state under the Bolsheviks. Because of its materialistic premises and primarily economic motivation, the Marxist system was essentially a cold and impersonal creed which roused strong emotions only in action as an aggressive protest against deeply suffered wrongs and as a common enterprise aiming, through the close co-operation of the masses, at the creation of a new and better society. This emotional and romantic side of Marxism is not to be felt in its ideas but in the social ferment which attempted to put these ideas in practice, to break the resistance offered by conservative institutions and to revivify society with a new set of goals, strivings and attachments. The role of Marxism in Russian revolutionary socialism is not dissimilar to that of dogmatic theology in the practice of religion. It has served as a foundation for a new confidence and as the justification for new destructive and creative impulses. It becomes living and vital, however, only in proportion as it is translated into concrete purposes, immediate feelings, and resolute and daring action.

The transformation of Marxism into a Russian way of life took place at a time when the latter was highly self-conscious and sensitive to the social implications of current economic trends. Industrialism had come to stay and industrialism brought with it inevitably and increasingly the accumulation of capital, and the growth of a proletariat. The influence of these factors on the stability of society in Western Europe was already luminously clear, and some Russian theorists envisaged a special type of social evolution in Russia by which the evils of competition between landed aristocracy and a monied *bourgeoisie* might be avoided and production might control distribution and its profits. Sociologists of the "subjectivist" school like Michailovski argued for the importance of individual leaders in social change, but tsarist Russia offered but a narrow field for the individual and the power of individuals could best be exercised through commitment to a dogmatic program which envisaged its own success in the inevitable operation of superpersonal economic and social forces. Marxism was such a creed par excellence and many of the most vigorous minds and daring adventurers of the 1880's and 1890's were prepared to embrace it and work for it. The earlier Russian Marxists, whether "orthodox" or "revisionist," were men of thought rather than action. Plekhanov, the leading pioneer and dogmatist of this school, was banished from Russia in 1880 and played no significant role in the realization of his own theories there. Lenin remained true to the philosophic tradition of his school, but he was more important as a leader than as a theorist and his successor Stalin has proved himself a brilliant and successful opportunist and administrator, but has added nothing to the history of ideas.

This shift of emphasis from thought to action coincided with the revolutionary years and the beginnings of the new state. The masses who flocked enthusiastically to the red banner of Bolshevism in the towns or succumbed to the steady pressure of the new regime in the country districts were concerned not with dialectic but with bread, land, and freedom from the oppressive landowners and wanted an unchallenged place of their own in the sun. The Revolution provided its own excitements and there was work for all. Initiative could be directed to immediate practical tasks under inspired and inspiring leaders; inquiring minds could find the formula for it all in the pages of Marx, Engels, and the Russian Marxists.

The experience of the Revolution and of the reconstruction of Russian society evoked fresh emotions and a different political and social orientation. A new patriotism emerged. Its heroes were Lenin and Stalin and local promoters of the Revolution throughout Russia and its associated republics. Its achievements were the new socialist state, the Soviet Constitution, the army, the new factories, and the collective farms. These persons and things established themselves both in the minds and hearts of the people and were not only accepted but roused lyrical enthusiasm. It was inevitable that this enthusiasm should seek creative outlet, particularly in poetry and folk tales.

Poetry about Lenin and Stalin forms a class by itself. On the whole there is little difference in motivation between the verses about Lenin and those about Stalin. Azadovskii observes, "For the popular bard to sing of Lenin means to glorify Stalin and to tell of Stalin means to magnify Lenin." There is recognition of Lenin's position as the pioneer leader of the Revolution and a less precise acknowledgment of his superior talents as a theorist in the frequent emphasis on his "wisdom." One obvious difference between the two men could, however, not be disregarded: the fact that Lenin is a dead hero, while Stalin is a live leader and administrator.

The death of Lenin was a profound shock to the sensibilities of his followers. Until Stalin had proved his competence as Lenin's successor, there was not only a great sense of loss but some uncertainty about the future. To offset this the poetry of this period about Lenin deals with his "immortality." These often quoted lines are typical:

Who says that Lenin's dead? He lives.
In generations new, he lives.
In the flowering of our youth, he lives.
In proletarian unity, he lives.
In world-wide revolution, still he lives.
In truth supreme which is our own, he lives.
In Spanish barricades, he lives.
Lenin is with us. That we know right well.
He lives.[2]

Many poems about Lenin and Stalin have little to do with the actual circumstances of their careers. Russian critics freely admit that these productions are not primarily biographical but are designed to express the emotions roused in the popular mind by the leaders. They form a kind of Soviet hagiography.

In defining the types of the great hero-leaders [writes Dymshitz], the popular poetry does not aim at a naturalistic realism, the circumstantiality of state records in the description of events, or photographic portraiture. Such naïve, empirical "realism" is foreign to folklore. The folklore of heroism takes a line directly opposite to this, the way of lyric-epic realism which does not pursue the external, imitative factors but conveys the significance and spiritual content of his achievement for his country and his native land by preserving the total, ideal value and spiritual richness of its hero. In the surface sketch of the hero and in his characteristic exploits, popular poetry does not hesitate to resort to the typical hyperbole of the heroic epic. In the development of its theme it does not hesitate occasionally to introduce motifs of fantasy and the fairy-tale. The realistic content of the folklore-product, however, does not lose one jot or tittle.

In popular poetry we shall not find an accurate factual portrait of either Lenin or Comrade Stalin. This problem does not concern the popular bard. He aims at reproducing broadly the wise humanity, the unprecedented daring of the great geniuses and revo-

[2] The original was composed in a dialect of Daghestan. Russian text in *Tvorchestvo narodov U.S.S.R.* Moscow, 1938. The English rendering is mine.

lutionaries of the present and for this he requires a truly epic setting. The popular bard describes the wisdom of Lenin and Stalin, their manner of life, all their achievements in relation to national life and the history of the peoples showing in it. He aims at presenting the leader's greatness, as it is reflected in the life and history of the working masses and he finds for this the only criterion relevant to his creative task; for their entire life, all their thoughts, their gigantic labor and the most subtle spiritual nuances of the leaders have been dedicated by them to the people.[3]

A similar statement is made by Azadovskii:

In the many tales composed in the early years of Soviet rule, and especially shortly after Lenin's death, it is impossible and inconsistent to look for a reflection of his actual portrait. This whole epos is not so much factual as an attempt to express and present in familiar terms the new world of sentiments and ideas, the new way of life which was introduced to the world by the name and figure of Lenin. It must be regarded as an attempt on the part of the working classes to preserve the heroic conflict through the medium of its witnesses and participants. A picture of Lenin, his work and teaching is drawn on a traditional pattern and this picture is the one which exerts a living influence on various social groups.

In these tales the name and figure of Lenin acquire the value of a symbol. It becomes the symbol of the heroic conflict, for freedom, the struggle for land. Through the legendary figure and legendary facade is reflected the image of the actual issue and the concrete struggle. Lenin does not simply assume the features and dress of earlier heroes and knights: within this outer casing lies a substance of a wholly new quality. The great exploits are the same but their meaning and point are quite different. Thus for example, in some folk-tales Lenin appears not merely as a hero but as the beggar-hero who struggles with evil and wrong. In an Ostyak song he comes in the traditional guise of a magic huntsman but his exploits have a different plot and point and are aimed at the prime enemies of the Ostyak workers, the exploiting merchant class. He kills the

[3] *Sovetskii Pholklor,* p. 98. Leningrad, 1939.

fur merchant and distributes to the poor the property of which they had been cheated.[4]

The principle involved here makes it easier to understand the spirit of the many poems, most of them of no great literary quality, which pay tribute to the local revolutionary leaders, to the symbols of industry and agriculture and to the home of the new proletariat, the large manufacturing towns and cities. Patrick has translated specimens of this genre which might be described as literature of cultural fervor, in distinction from the literature of patriotic fervor discussed above, though obviously no sharp line of division can be drawn between the two.

The following three illustrations are taken from the literary output of a once backward agricultural district in the Caucasus, Kakhetia, which was visited in 1936 by the Georgian folklorist Chkhaidze.

How excellent is this age!

How excellent is the age in which we live,
Adorned with many colors bright.
Both old and young rejoice with all their hearts.
Collective farms hold undisputed sway.
A mammoth harvest reaped is stored away.
High powered tractors serve appointed tasks,
Threshing machines add power mechanized,
The reaping and the threshing mechanically devised.
The grain cries to the reaper
    "Come on, lad, make it faster."
The combines greet their founders joyfully.
We used to harness buffalo to threshing carts
Their tongues hung out while they strained at the load.
Some fell upon the threshing floor.
Their drivers beat them cutting through their hide.
In ignorance dark we gaped at new machines.

[4] M. Azadovskii, *Sovetskaya Pholkloristika za 20 Let. Sovetskii Pholklor VI,* 1939, p. 20.

Before when people spoke to us of them
They seemed to us like fabled monsters of romance
And when we saw the tractors then we learned
That they would really do our ploughing well.
In former times our peasants pulled the plough
Which made the even furrows in the soil.
They got their oxen ready and their rods
Tough knotted cut the flanks of weary beasts.
They beat them striking even at their eyes.
How excellent is the age in which we live.
Stalin we thank for this our joyful life.

—Sandro Chiboschvili, 1937.[5]

I love you, tractor mine!

I love you, tractor mine,
I love your voice.
You're faster than all else, it's very clear.
In ploughing, you surpass ten pair of oxen.
You plough, you mow, you've earned yourself a name in harvest
 time.
How well you thresh the wheat and light the peasant's home.
The peasant puts aside his oily lamp,
He bears no more the cost of kerosene.
The whole collective farm gives you its love,
Your fame has spread among us far and wide.
Our thanks are due to Stalin for this boon,
Our way was dark. He shed upon it light.

—Joseph Hohashvili, 1936.[6]

The Red Army

I am the son of the working people,
I am the son of the Army Red.
My tent is my love and I love it dearly;
My training will serve me, I know, in good stead.

[5] *Sovetskii Pholklor* VI, p. 116, 1939. The English rendering is mine.
[6] *Ibid.*, p. 118. The English rendering is mine.

Firmly I stand at my post
And my eyes do not waver to right or left.
I fear no foe in the world.
A pleasure 'twill be to test my arms,
My rifle, my pistol, my hand grenade.

Our enemies serve us as welcome meat.
We gnaw at their bones and throw them away.
With passion we fight for our native lands,
Their governments rest in our own strong hands.
We are Red fighters of stubborn steel.
Sons of the working people, we
Are joined in undying loyalty.
    —Joseph Hohashvili, 1936.[7]

The first two poems are peculiarly instructive in registering
the sentiments of the local population toward the changes introduced into local methods of farming by Soviet rule. In the
first the note of warm humanity is conspicuous and includes
within its range not only the beasts which once dragged the
farmer's plough but even nature itself which responds to the
peasant's need to exploit it.

> The grain cries to the reaper,
> "Come on, lad, make it faster."

In the poem on the tractor there is a sense of practical realism about the advantages of mechanical equipment. The tractor
not only does the work but provides light which obviates the
inconveniences of the old kerosene lamps. The poem on the
Red Army is typical but is remarkable in coming from so remote a region of the U.S.S.R. Here again the emphasis on the
new mechanical equipment has the same lyrical quality.

> A pleasure 'twill be to test my arms,
> My rifle, my pistol, my hand grenade.

[7] *Ibid.*, p. 120. The English rendering is mine.

A remarkably large proportion of contemporary patriotic literature in the U.S.S.R. is the work of the Ukrainian, Armenian, Georgian, Azerbaijanian, and even Kurdish authors. In a collection of poems extolling the new Soviet order and entitled *The Stalin Constitution in the Poetry of the Nations of the U.S.S.R.,* the majority are translations.

The works of modern Armenian poets offer especially dramatic testimony to the new spirit in view of the fierce nationalism of the Armenians and their passionate struggle against all forms of foreign domination.

Revolutionary conditions [writes the latest historian of Armenian poetry], led to a re-grouping among the Armenian intelligentsia. One section, hostile to the nation, stuck in the bog of the emigrant Tashnags. Another better group headed by the great national poet Ovanes Tumanean opened its arms to the Soviet rule. Together with Tumanean, Shirvanzadye, Ovanes Joanissean, Isaacean, Nar-Dos, Demirchean and others took their place in Soviet literature.

The victory of Soviet power in Armenia made possible the idea of Armenian-Soviet poetry. The wise national policy of the party of Lenin and Stalin brought new life to Armenian art, more particularly literature and poetry. In spite of all the idle "prophecies" of the enemies of Soviet arts about the decline and extinction of folklore and the poetry of the Ashugs, we have seen exactly the opposite take place. Inspired by the ideas of the socialist revolution and the establishment of Communism in our country, Soviet Armenian poetry has been a powerful weapon in the struggle to establish a new society. Like all the international poetry of the peoples of the U.S.S.R. it has exhibited a new quality, the most advanced in the world. The drift of its ideas has been determined by the movement toward Communism; the richness of its themes is derived from the new life which has inspired it, and its significance lies in its development of individuality in our land.[8]

The obvious bias of this account is its most instructive feature. The two following poems illustrate its meaning. The first

[8] *Antologiya Armyanskoi Poezii,* p. 32. Moscow, 1942.

was composed in 1904 by Akon Akonean, one of the earliest Armenian Communist poets and describes the pathos of the class struggle, which in Armenia was closely associated with the struggle for national independence:

Meum et Tuum

Wandering through the gay bazaar
I paused idly at a stall
At his hearth the silversmith
Struck his anvil, fanned the flame.

There beneath the raining blows
Writhed the molten silver mass.
Bitterly in fright it cried
Till the smith cast it aside.

Idly to another shop
Wandered I past friendly doors,
Over metal crucibles
Worked the jeweller with zeal.

And beneath the iron hammer
Weeping, quails the golden mass
Grief with unavailing sigh
Greets the idle passer-by.

Further on I meet a blacksmith
Mighty strikes the hammer there
And the heavy mass of metal
Loudly groans its protest vain.

And beneath the heavy blows
'Neath the hammer's heavy beating
Casts its sparks like flaming prayers
In a flaming circle round it.

Then I asked though idly strolling,
"What's the meaning of this, brother?

Silver have I seen in tears
Beaten, writhing, all exhausted.

"Gold was groaning, as the master
Workman cut its breast with cunning stroke,
Even you, O powerful iron
Cried, aloud your pain. Now why?

"You are stronger, you are blacker
Than the smithy's glowing coals,
Can you suffer then more deeply
Than the silver and the gold?"

"I will give an honest answer
To your fair and honest words
Truly is my anguish greater
Than the silver's and the gold's."

Thus the iron gave his answer
"Different is their lot in kind
Other metal tears their substance
But my brother strikes at me."

Worthy comrade, give some thought here.
Greater anguish cannot be
Than when brother strikes at brother,
Kin yet mortal enemy.[9]

The temper of this poem is romantic and passive and its
emotional quality literary and stylized. In sharp contrast is the
poem "My Native Land" written in 1939 by Azat Vshtuni, a
native of Van, in which the natural beauties of Armenia are
enumerated in conventional fashion but with a sense of emancipation long absent from Armenian verse. The social scene is
now in harmony with nature itself and it is this combination
which makes his country appear incomparable to the poet.

[9] *Ibid.*, p. 551. The English rendering is mine.

Such sentiments as the four lines below are familiar enough:

Mother country! Your like is not found in the great world
Yours are the stately forests, vast expanse of steppe and mountain
    range
Rushing rivers and the singing waves of sea and azure lakes.
In golden fields, in whispering groves, your voice eternal sounds.

But a new note is struck in the lines:

> The busy hum of factories now is heard
> Men glow with labor's fire.
> A valiant band of daring youth
> Is full of staunch good will.
> The past is buried deep,
> The sad old world destroyed without a trace.
> Breathe freely, country mine, advance.
> You have no equal now.
> Full many tribes in freedom live
> And sing their songs in vale and mountain slope
> They sing of Stalin, glorious leader, bold
> In many a dialect strange the tale is told.
> His name's a flaming banner,
> Gleaming emblem of our hopes
> On paths in every district of our land.
> Oh, country mine. You have no equal now.[10]

Poets like this do not look to the past for a golden age. **Ovanes**
Shiraz, one of the younger generation, wrote in 1935:

> The old world is unknown to me
> I knew it not in youth.
> What would recall it to me
> Out of the obscurity of dust and murk?
> But when I look
> Into my gray-haired mother's eyes
> It rises menacing with death, and filth and misery replete.

[10] *Ibid.*, p. 573. The English rendering is mine.

The old world is unknown to me
I knew it not in youth
But in the dimming pupils of her eyes
Its mists do hover still.[11]

Three poets stand out with special prominence among the
Soviet bards for their individual genius: Marfa Semënovna
Kryukova, Dzhambul Dzhavaev, and Suleiman Stalskii. All
come from remote regions of the Soviet Union; all are minstrels who improvise, not write, and all have carried over the
tradition of minstrelsy from prerevolutionary times into the
new world of Soviet achievement.

Marfa Semënovna Kryukova was born in Nizhnyaya Zimn-
yaya Zolotitsa, a colony of Novgorod, in the province of Archangel on the White Sea, in 1875. Her family, like most of the
inhabitants of the region, were boatmen and fishermen and for
three generations had produced gifted minstrels. Marfa went
to the village school where she developed a passion for reading.
Political exiles assigned to her village took an interest in her
development and lent her books. From them and from the oral
epic tradition of the neighborhood she found themes for her
compositions. Her remarkable talents were no discovery of the
Soviet folklorists but had been recognized by Markov on his
anthropological expedition to Archangel, 1898–1901. A number
of her pieces were transcribed and published in the reports of
this expedition.

In 1937 a similar expedition was sent to this region by the
Government Literary Museum under the direction of Borodiva
and Lipets. A careful study of Kryukova's work was made and
two stout volumes of her earlier poems, some 1,500 pages, were
published. In 1938 she was elected to membership in the Union
of Soviet Authors. She made appearances in Moscow and other
cities, spoke over the radio, and gave recitals. In 1939 she was

[11] *Ibid.*, p. 627. The English rendering is mine.

decorated with the Order of the Workers' Red Flag. She was pensioned and established in a new house in her native village where she still lives and works.

The earlier verse of Kryukova embodies the traditional heroic themes: Ilya Mavromets and Dobryna. Shorter poems on a long series of historical personages running through the Middle Ages and down to modern times: Vladimir the Great, Prince Michael, Ivan the Terrible, Peter the Great, and even Menshikov. Since her recognition by the Soviet public Kryukova has improvised on modern themes: a poem describing the revolutionary movements under Lenin's guidance, a lament over Lenin, a panegyric on Stalin, "Stalin's glory will be eternal," a political poem on "Rockbuilt Moscow," another on Chapai's march on Moscow.

The connecting link between these compositions dealing with such different times and persons is the intense patriotic feeling of the composer and the curious manner in which she carries over the old epic types and techniques into the treatment of the Soviet world. Soviet critics make much of the way in which the contrast between the nobles and beggars in folklore plots reflect the class struggles, but actually there is no real consciousness of class struggles in the earlier productions. The rise of the poor hero to riches and honor is a theme common to all such poetry. The pathos is personal and individual, not social. The exalted beggar becomes a capitalist and an aristocrat in the end. Only after Kryukova's imagination had been fired by her concert tours and wide acquaintance with the new order, did she make its themes and drama her own.

The same is true of the other two Soviet bards, Dzhambul Dzhavaev and Suleiman Stalskii. The former was born in 1849 in the province of Kazakestan north of Afghanistan, a country of mountains and wild steppes. Here capital was in the hands not of land owners and industrialists, but the rich merchants who controlled the bazaars and trade routes, and the atheistic campaign must drive at mullahs, mosques, and the teaching of the Koran. As in northern Siberia, the native literature of this region was epic and consisted mainly in the improvisation of bards and minstrels on heroic themes, such as the invasion of the Tatars and the annexation of Kazakestan by Ivan the Terrible. Muchtar Auezov observes:

> It may be deduced from the fact that the heroes (of the earliest epic poems) are not Kazaks but "descendants of the Nogaili," that the original variations of the heroic poems arose at a time when the independent Kazak political union had not yet taken shape, when the tribes which form the ethnic substratum of the Kazak people, still belonged to the Golden Horde, the khanates of the Crimea and Kazan, and passed under the general, more popular name "Nogaili."[12]

The authors of the earliest poems are unknown and no certain attributions of authorship can be made before the end of the eighteenth century. In the nineteenth century written literature developed side by side with the still flourishing oral tradition. In 1822 the territory was annexed by Russia and arrangement led to periodic popular revolts, and the exploits of local heroes are recounted by the minstrels and bards. In the second half of the nineteenth century the best authors came under Russian influence, notably Abaya Kunanbaeva (1845–1905) who is credited with founding the modern school of poetry and moulding a Kazak literary language. The most talented of all Kazak poets is, however, Dzhambul Dzhavaev. Though born in the year 1849 Dzhambul's best-known work falls in the Soviet period and forms part of the cultural development of that country under Bolshevik rule. Probably his most remarkable poem is one on his own life. It opens:

Song flourished in the century past.
Though national minstrelsy is ageless, so we think,

[12] *Antologiya Kazakhskoi Literatury*, p. 11. Moscow, 1940.

The people do not lose their native song
Death does not terminate harmonious melody.
Song and the heart live close in friendship bound
Song and the heart with happiness resound.

The centuries whirl by,
Songs of the steppe recall this fact to me.
I watch the seeker of a happy human lot
Press forward to horizons endless; endless quest.
My steppe has known of Asan Kaig
The songs of Asan perished in the sands.

The centuries whirl by,
Songs of the steppe recall this fact to me.
My people saddled a magic carpet
Poised like a falcon for its winged flight
Higher than Ala-tai's most lofty peaks
The Kazak people dreamed to make ascent.

The centuries whirl by,
The bitterness of life recalls this fact to me.
A dry, harsh wind has lashed against my heart
My dream has withered.
Dzhambul is mute and cannot sing in his loved haunts of old.

Legends and stories have I stored in mind
And carried them in travels far and wide.
I look: my song is borne across a frightful precipice
Like a proud eagle in its giddy flight.
Shota appears, the people's champion,
Erect and tall like Kazak's pearly heights.
The proud and fiery son of Georgian hills,
I see him go alone through vale and gorge.
A mist arises on the hills like smoke.
He strides along the panther's trail
And carries in his breast songs of the people, love and dreams,
Keeping himself forever young.

I see the timorous reptiles slither past,
I hear the flashing, singing waterfalls.
They wish to smother with cold foam
The flaming song, the turbulent spirit's strain.
The champion, however, warm beneath his panther skin,
Hurries along to cheer the people with his well-loved song.

The centuries whirl by,
Songs of the steppe recall this fact to me.
The heat burns the thick grass,
The caravan proceeds along its trackless way,
The desert winds whip up the sand,
The storm now follows in the caravan's wake,
The weary camel softly treads its path.
On sandy wastes the rider does not sing,
Tears in his eyes, blood on his lips
Taras, beloved singer of Ukraine,
Travels along on camel back.

The centuries whirl by.
Taras is traveling on a camel's back,
His lips are tightly closed; he does not sing.
Anguished he sees his people yoked as slaves,
His song lies heavy on his heart,
A double-headed eagle circles monstrous in the sky.
Like faithful folk we followed in the ambling tracks of Taras.
Thirst made us weary and the sand was dust.
Bright gleamed our bayonets and shoulder straps,
Endless the dunes heaped up by wind and storm.
The minstrel's song is lost among the dunes.

The centuries whirl by.
Pushkin appears in simple garb,
His cart is rickety, the wheels creak rustily,
The joints and broken wooden collar screech.
Crows circle in formation black.
The minstrel's anguished heart is retched with pain.

The rumbling cart bears the poet on,
Good Pushkin sings the people's song.
The tsar's afraid, the people joyful now.
Pushkin's a wanderer, like our own bard Kaig.
He sings the greatness of the Russian folk
From Kazak's wild and snowy heights.
His voice is carried far and wide;
It seems its melody will never die.
It breathes in Abai's spirit
And on gray Tyan-Shanya
In golden language native to Kazak.

The centuries whirl by.
Dzhambul is moving through his country dear
And like an eagle on Caucasian slopes
Never departing from his appointed course
He spreads his spirit's wings.
He does not bend his back before the beys
Inspired by the glory of his name.

He is no bard, who does not call to arms
Who does not live committed in his heart to his own fold,
Who does not sing the songs of his own land.
Sing, poets, and make our land resplendent
Like the eternal glory of the Kremlin make it shine,
Like the distinction of that man
With whom the world has sung the brotherhood of man,
Stalin the nation's dream, their joy and prize,
Stalin beloved of all with equal none,
Stalin the poet of this great planet wide,
Stalin the singer of the people's songs,
Stalin the mighty sire of Dzhambul.[13]

As in Kryukova's work, the interesting feature of this poem
is the ingenious way in which the bard makes the transition
from the earlier Kazak culture to the Soviet era, indicating in

[13] *Ibid.*, p. 445. The English rendering is mine.

passing the formative influence of Russian liberalism upon the literature of his country. Similar procedures can be traced in all the literatures of the U.S.S.R. in the Lezgin verses of Suleiman Stalskii, among the Armenian and Georgian nationalists and in the tales and songs of the remote Caucasian tribes of Chechnya and Ingushetia. How easily the minstrel himself can become a heroic figure is shown in a Ukrainian story, published in the collection, *Gnyevnoe Slovo,* which describes Taras Bulba risking his life by wandering in German occupied territory with his guitar, brutally blinded by the Germans but succeeding in stealing crucial plans from the headquarters of the German general staff.

It has been possible to reproduce here only a few typical examples of the literature of patriotic and cultural fervor. This is less to be regretted, however, as the variety of this material is not comparable to its bulk and there is a uniformity in the treatment of stock themes. The emotions expressed are common emotions and are expressed in common terms. Their literary expressions, therefore, for the most part lack the savor of individuality. There are some exceptions, but most of the tales and poems are obviously "situational" and have demanded a minimum of personal creative genius.

The main importance of this literature lies, therefore, in its content and still more in its social function. It is a product of the ferment of a new Russian age but it is itself a powerful leaven. It inspires achievement with romance, hard work with sentiment, and the common enterprise with a poetic creed. It is a unifying and constructive force.

All these things seem evident to Russian readers, but questions occur to the critical outsider of which the most obvious is, "Is this literature sincere and spontaneous or is it a product direct or indirect of a clever and deeply penetrating propaganda? Are the modern bards real minstrels who sing because that is their nature and who stand in the long line of poet-prophets who perceive the drift and sense the meaning of thier age and interpret it in homely idiom to their fellows? Or are they a subtle brand of agent who have for one reason or another placed their gifts and their wares at the disposal of the Communist bureau of propaganda?"

Undoubtedly the literature of political and cultural fervor is a literature of converts. The literature of protest is found, for obvious reasons, only among the Russian emigrants, just as the literature of protest against the tsarist regime was produced in the old days, for the most part, abroad. It should, however, be recognized that the conversion is, at least in the majority of cases, genuine. The quality of the poetic feeling leaves no possibility of doubt about that. Its forms of expression may at times be second rate but its inspiration is not at second hand. A great poet might hesitate to sing of kerosene lamps but an insincere poet would be overconscious of its impropriety.

Part of the answer to the psychological problem of the new folk literature lies in the rapidity with which cultural change has been effected in the U.S.S.R. Soviet education has reached an incredible high in an amazingly short time but it started from what, to our Western notions, was an inconceivable low in vast areas of the Soviet Union. In these areas the bards and minstrels, like the early prophets of Israel, were not only the visionaries but also the reporters and critics of contemporary life. Their technique was that of popular entertainment. They sang rhythmically, romantically, passionately but also shrewdly. The wisdom of the court buffoons, the *smorochi,* often exceeded the wisdom of their court listeners.

This tradition, which in Western Europe was supplemented by the printed book and the more sophisticated literary genres, never died out and never was replaced in many thousand square miles of Soviet territory where the language of the people until recent days had not been reduced to writing. The surprising amount of non-Russian Soviet literature is not due merely to the desire on the part of official Communism to present a united front among the nations within its federation, nor to the not insignificant fact that Stalin himself is no Russian but a Georgian by birth and education. It is due mainly to the fact that on the broad steppes of northern and central Russia and in the mountains of the Caucasus and Armenia the natural response to cultural change was in song and story. The bards and minstrels of the Middle Ages were neither detached observers nor impartial critics. They sang quite literally for their supper and drifted with all their quizzicalness and penetrating humor with the tide of human events. Their business was and is to capture the mood of the time and to make of it romance, whether it be the romance of feudalism and knight-errantry or of leaders, factories, farms, and machinery. In this respect the impulse of propaganda and the impulse of response to propaganda are parts of the same process, the conversion of one sixth of the world's surface to a new way of life, a way which leads from buffaloes to tractors and threshing machines, from ignorance to literacy, and from the political frustration and oppression of working men to their responsible participation in the affairs of government.

It can be seen from this sampling how amply justified Russian folklorists have been in collecting and publishing this new material, which reflects so vividly the psychological aspects of the Soviet cultural revolution. The political significance of this literature and its potential usefulness in the campaign against religion is no less apparent, for it breathes a secular piety which in the view of Communist leaders should replace the traditional pieties of Christianity, Judaism and Mohammedanism, and unite the sentiments of all citizens of the U.S.S.R. in a cult of heroes and new institutions. Unlike the reforms of Augustus or the fanatical revival of Shintoism in Japan, this secular piety does not depend on a revival of the past but a lively concern with the present. The past serves only as a reservoir of feeling and emotional forms adaptable without break of continuity to the needs of contemporary life.

The historian should never play the prophet and one must be content to conclude our account of Russian religion with a brief analysis of its present inconclusive phase. The success or failure of the campaign to mobilize the drive behind the new folklore of achievement and make of it a substitute for religion will depend ultimately upon its capacity to absorb impulses which in the past have found expression in religion.

The limitations of the new literature are the limitations of the ideology which produced it, and reflect the transitional character of the time. There are no cosmic perspectives, no limiteless horizons. All is conquest, achievement and practical results. Man is judged by what he can do, not by what he is. There is no real consolation for physical weakness and human failure and no value latent in tragedy and suffering. There is no concern for ultimates. This is true not only of the proletariat but of the agricultural workers as well. In spite of Patrick's plea for the continuity of Russian popular poetry, there is a great difference in poise and repose and in the acceptance of a life as a whole between 1915 and 1935.

To the cosmic sense the Communist theory gives no satisfactory response. It cannot be imagined that the speech of the scout leader, in the play quoted earlier, about eternal motion and the domination of universal space by man will in the long run and in the light of sober experience stir the minds and wills of many. The difficulty here is that paradoxically religion can lag behind science in its account of the outside world but cannot ignore inner realities. The cosmic sense projects its own contents from primitive needs which are ultimately biological and social. Mere achievement does not satisfy all those needs and the surplus which achievement cannot absorb is left for religion to express. The secular thought and piety of Communism thwarts this output or else, as in the cruder materialistic cosmologies, gives it more fanciful form than theology.

We hear very little of pain and frustration in Soviet literature. Just as in its scientific view the search for values is brushed aside or dismissed with glib formulae, so the problem of individual destiny is swallowed up in the whole or beclouded by larger social issues. Visitors to Russian hospitals and deathbeds report a stoicism and patience highly characteristic of the Russian temperament, but in the last analysis the sufferers are left out of the picture. They have no place in Utopia.

In this regard the war has materially altered the situation. Evil has become personal. Suffering, disability, death and loss are no longer the peculiar lot of a socially insignificant minority, but a common and intense experience. In meeting this together many Russians have been thrown back on older and more primitive securities: older in point of time and more basic in the emotional economy of human nature. It is against this pattern of man's insuperable limitations that the limited validity and applicability of the Communist view of life has become most apparent to the Russians themselves. The millions of rubles contributed to the defense fund by the Church when it would have been more acceptable to the state through any other channel is significant in this regard.

One may well ask how long the present mood of strenuousness can last and the answer is probably: As long as there is much work to be done and a vigorous and unified interest sustained in doing it. This cannot in the nature of things be for long, as history is reckoned. There are already stirrings of unrest stimulated and fortified by the pressures of war. Religion has revived and Stalin's early theological training may have convinced him that the only hope of controlling and utilizing religion is by tolerating it. Religious toleration, however, means the toleration of a rival ideology and a moral ethos divergent from the official philosophy of materialism. It is a question vital for the future culture of Russia whether popular sentiment will be satisfied with the new folklore as an expression of its deepest needs. If so, a new religion will arise in Russia; if not, a return to Christianity may be expected. In any case it is certain that the popular mind will be led by folklore to the roots of folklore, the unconscious intimations and insights of a superpersonal, supersocial, and supernatural order.

The most important practical question for the future of religion is whether Russian youth are or will be religious and if so, what form their religion will take. The evidence here is scattered and unsatisfactory and Soviet literature is a highly suspect source. The complaints by the atheistical groups against the apathy of the Komsomol in the campaign for godlessness, the witness of observers that youth attended churches in large numbers in the years immediately preceding the war should not be overlooked. The pictures of congregations given in *The Truth about Religion in Russia* show mostly women and old men, but the young men were at the front and in the training camps and a grudging concession was wrung from the government that soldiers who carried crosses and icons in their kits were not to be censured. Their sacrifice entitled them to this indulgence.

Doubts are often expressed about the sincerity of the government in making such allowances and of the new tolerance toward what appears to be a revival of religious faith and practice on a wide scale. The answer is probably that the policy of the government is cynical but realistic. An important paragraph, the significance of which has been neglected, appears in the instructions issued by the Communist party on the treatment of the religious question in 1926:

A particularly important condition to the success of antireligious propaganda, as of every agitational and cultural-educational activity, is its strict co-ordination with the conditions and peculiarities of a given moment.

At present we observe, in the toiling masses, two opposite processes in the field of religious experience. On the one hand, religion is exhausting itself, and atheism is spreading and deepening; this progress is seen in the growth of the Society of Atheists and the increasing rejection of religious ceremonies (baptisms, church weddings, and funerals, and the entertainment of the priest on feast days), as well as an increased interest in antireligious lectures and literature. On the other hand, in some strata of the toiling population, not only among peasants but also among workers, is observed the opposite process, an increasing growth in some places of sectarianism, in others a strengthening of Orthodox parishes.

Antireligious propaganda must be construed upon an exact computation and scientific Marxian grasp of all the peculiarities of the given moment, on which background such contradictory phenomena as the growth of atheism and the strengthening of religion are comprehensible. Antireligious propaganda must proceed from a clear understanding "of the social roots" of religion precisely now, at the given period of socialist construction and must be closely related to the political tasks of the moment. The growth of atheism, generally speaking, is conditioned by the very process of socialist construction. The participation of the toiling masses in the administration of the state, in the trade union and co-operative movement, in political educational work, in the growth of agriculture, of technique and of co-operation in the villages, etc.—all such participation conditions the desertion of religion by the working masses. But inasmuch as socialist construction (even though in the form of agricultural producers co-operation) does not yet sufficiently embrace the broad peasant masses, and inasmuch as the poor and middle peasant still remains an individual small producer, in so far the premises of religious sentiment are for the time preserved in these strata, in the economic conditions of their existence. These sentiments are also upheld in the backward strata of the proletariat, among petty artisans and similar groups of toilers, by the comparatively high cost of living, by unemployment, by insufficient organization of this strata, and by the inadequacy of educational work among them. In this respect those new working strata, formed by peasants migrating for work to the towns without severing their relation to the village, also demand attention. However, the increased activity of priests and sectarian leaders at the present time is undoubtedly due not so much to the maintenance of religious sentiment in the various strata of the working population as to the development of the new *bourgeoisie* (the *kulaks* in the villages and the *nepmen* in the cities). *Kulaks* and *nepmen* make use of religion in new forms, under changed circumstances, for their class interests. Antireligious propaganda must take into consideration the new forms of class utilization by the *kulaks* of the religious sentiments of the middle and poor peasants, in order thus to counteract the aims of socialist construction in the villages. Therefore antireligious propaganda must be construed so as to be closely related to the general work of the socialist construction of the Party and Soviet power, and also with the problems and methods of this work under present conditions.[14]

Mutatis mutandis, it may be surmised that the policy of the Communist leaders remains in principle unchanged and the remarks about *kulaks* and *nepmen* would now be replaced by war considerations.

For those who believe that religion is a wholesome ferment in human life and culture, the brightest hopes are held out by the progress of Orthodoxy, under Tikhon, Peter, Sergius and Alexei. These are the men who represent the main line of Russian religious tradition, who have stayed at home and have done the work, and who have pursued a policy of effective compromise, not of principle, but between initiative and restraint. Much has depended in the last twenty-five years on accurate timing and great patience in maintaining and advancing Church life. The greatest credit for masterful strategy in this respect must go to the Patriarch Sergius.

Second in importance to the continuance of Orthodoxy is the

[14] Hecker, *op. cit.,* p. 277.

future of the autonomous national churches and the Roman Church, the survival of the sects and the continued hold of Judaism and Mohammedanism in different parts of the Soviet Union. It seems wholly unlikely that Roman Catholicism will sweep Russia or that the present government will encourage its expansion. Its hold on Polish and Ukrainian elements has been weakened like the hold of Orthodoxy upon Russians, by the same means and as part of the same official policy. Its recovery, however, will be rendered more difficult by the lack of both government and popular support, though much here may depend on the future of Russian-Polish relations. The strategy of the Papacy in Russia since the Revolution has been singularly maladroit. The political and social instincts and interests of the Roman Church appear to have prevented clear vision and opportune action. Open war with Bolsheviks was declared precipitately and has hopelessly compromised *rapprochement* between the Soviet state and the Vatican.

The future of Protestantism in Russia is still more uncertain. Protestantism is not the religion of Russians as a whole and makes no convincing appeal to Russian religious instinct. Soviet critics have been in a sense right in associating denominational efforts with the *bourgeoisie,* for it has flourished mainly among the enterprising, hardworking farming and trading classes. This class has now been almost entirely assimilated to the Communist organization of agriculture and business. The lines between different Protestant groups have always been more flexible than in other countries and it is not surprising to hear of a recent amalgamation of the Baptists and Evangelicals. For the moment some ground is firmly held, but even more than with the Roman Church, outside help has been required and the future of Protestantism in Russia seems to depend on the future political relations of Russia with countries like England, America, and even Germany.

The native Russian sects may die out but their disappearance will be gradual and in the nature of the case they will be replaced. Exotic sects are the inevitable accompaniments of great religions. They ride the trough of the wave but they represent the dissident spirit in man which neither revolution nor stabilization will in the long run affect. The fate of Judaism and Mohammedanism is not yet clear.

With regard to the future of Anglo-Orthodox relations in Russia, these are likely to prosper if Anglo-Catholicism continues to gain strength in the Church of England and the Episcopal Church in America, and if Russian Orthodoxy can extend its principle of *oikonomia* to admit Anglican claims to purity of faith, valid orders, and an effective sacramental system. Here too the role of politics may not be inconsiderable. The relations between Russia and England and America will greatly facilitate or greatly impede any working arrangement between the churches. In the last analysis, however, ecclesiastical agreement can only be reached with profit in the religious sphere.

If we may provisionally concede an effective renaissance to Russian Orthodoxy, it must be recognized that its survival has been largely due to the lessons learned in the years of bitter persecution. Although Communist critics ignored the religious content and issues presented by the Church, they were quite right in seeing in the institution a vehicle of class feeling and a powerful support for the stratification of society in an imperial state. The ecclesiastics of the old school were the least inclined to relinquish this as one of the functions of Orthodoxy in society. With the emergence of a more liberal economy and a more representative government the Church was poorly adapted and conspicuously unadaptable to the new order of things. Patronage, not accomplishment, and sanctified privilege rather than hallowed labor, had been her props for many centuries. In coming to terms with the new state, Orthodoxy came ready to meet the moral demand of the new age.

The survival of the Church has, however, depended not only on her own adroit shift of ground but on the stubborn persistence of religion as a factor in human life. This has run counter to earlier Communist convictions, and Russian atheists have accepted Communist dogma more readily than the facts. The continued revival of religion will be greatly facilitated by the interest, sympathy, and co-operation of Christian countries with whom Russia may stand in friendly relation, but the growth of religion on Russian soil is indigenous and whether circumstances favor the Church or work against her, she has toughened her resistance, disciplined her body, and sharpened her wits for future effort. She has learned to feed her flock in lean pastures and to guard it with her pastoral staff from ravening wolves. In harmony with her own people through sharing their life she can at last say with assurance, *In mundo pressuram habebitis; sed confidite, ego vici mundum.*

EPILOGUE

SINCE THE FOREGOING CHAPTERS WERE written, events in Russian Church history have moved rapidly. Co-operation between Church and State has grown much closer in practice. An All-Russian Church council has been held and a new patriarch elected. A substantial part of the confiscated Church property has been given back. Churches and shrines have been restored to public worship. Some seventy monasteries are now functioning. Seminaries have been reopened, notably the important centers of theological learning at Kiev, Kazan, Moscow, and Leningrad. The patriarchate has been permitted initiative in unifying the Church at home and abroad. Conversations have taken place between Moscow and emigrant groups distrustful of the Mother Church under Soviet rule. Attempts have been made to heal the wounds of schism in Paris, in Yugoslavia, and in the United States. The group under Bishop Eulogius in Paris has resumed relations with the Patriarch of Moscow. The Serbian faction bound by the resolutions of the Synod of Karlowitz has followed suit. Negotiations with American Orthodoxy have proved more delicate and complicated, but after some false starts they are still under way. Relations are being cemented between the Russian Church and religious bodies who have been solicitous of Russian religious life abroad and helpful in maintaining its structure. Archbishop Alexei of Rostov and Yaroslav has visited the United States as the representative of Patriarch Alexei.

There have been consultations with the Federal Council of Churches, officers of the Y.M.C.A., and with bishops of the Episcopal Church. Visits to Russia by the Archbishop of York and the pro-Soviet dean of Canterbury have been welcomed, greetings have been exchanged, and return visits paid. For obvious reasons, the Anglican and Episcopal Churches are in positions of strategic advantage in these negotiations, the present aims of which have yet to be clarified. Unfortunately the situation between the Russian Orthodox and Roman Catholic Churches has deteriorated rather than improved. Memories of Spain and Italy are still fresh in Russian minds.

To bring the story up to date the following points must be discussed: (1) the recent relations between Church and State in Russia; (2) the results of the *sobor* held in Moscow on January 31, 1945; (3) the question of unity within the Russian Church at home and abroad; and (4) the outcome of extra-Orthodox relations with Anglicans, Protestants, and Roman Catholics.

1. On October 8, 1943 the Council of People's Commissars established a Soviet Council on Orthodox Affairs to work with the Soviet Commission on Religious Cults. The new council was headed by Mr. G. G. Karpov and included three assistants, C. A. Zaitev, S. T. Utkin, and I. I. Ivanov, and also an executive secretary. In an interview to the Religious News Service, Mr. Karpov thus described the work of his committee:

Our Council was set up by the Council of People's Commissars on October 8, 1943, and since then we have gained a fair amount of experience. We have had no friction, and every complaint has been attended to. Our basic task is to maintain contact between the government and the Church. This was done first through the late Patriarch Sergius, and is now being done through Acting Patriarch Alexei and the Orthodox Synod. We have established our representatives in all regions, provinces, and republics of the Soviet Union. We now have more than a hundred, and they all devote full time to this work. They, in turn, have their representatives in the local soviets, and these maintain contact with local church affairs.

The most important work of the council appears to have been the opening of theological seminaries. Ten were ordered to open by August 1, 1945 by Karpov's council. Permission was first granted for the reopening of the theological institute at Moscow but has been followed by leave to begin courses in the seminary at Saratov. Later, similar permits were issued for the ancient foundations of Kiev and Kazan and for seminaries at Minsk, Odessa, Stavropol, Lvov, Lutzk, and Tallinn. The reason for this change of policy is not hard to guess. In the period before the war when the program of the atheistical groups was that of the Communist party and was supported by the government, it was the avowed intention of the authorities to cut the life of the Church at its source by preventing training to the priesthood. As the clergy then alive died off there would be no new ones to take their place and the practice of religion would gradually be rendered impossible. It was known that training centers for the Russian clergy operated outside Russia, and it was understood that men trained abroad might arrange surreptitiously to enter Russia and take up their duties there. These means could hardly have been successful in the long run as the number of such priests was necessarily very small and the chances of exercising their ministry when they arrived were extremely hazardous.

Once the government decided to tolerate religion, it was important that it should also regulate it. The political sympathies of the emigrant groups in Paris and elsewhere were prevailingly conservative and often anti-Soviet. Men trained abroad were therefore likely to feel, if not to act, as enemies of the state and in any case would be alien to the new Russian social order. At best their contribution to contemporary Russian society would be negligible, at worst subversive. Inside Russia the patriarchal Church had shown a spirit of realistic compromise and a desire to integrate Christianity with Soviet patriotism. It was obviously better, if the Church had come to stay, to see that its hierarchy was reared in this atmosphere and stood behind these principles. The establishment of the Soviet Council on Orthodox Affairs was in part a recognition and ratification of the new relations between Church and State, in part a safeguard from the government that the Soviet law should be observed in letter and in spirit. The personnel of the council includes no ecclesiastics, only Soviet officials. It is a government agency designed to gauge and control the expansion of the Church in accordance with the wishes of the state. Mr. Karpov in his interview also stated:

Church and State are separated in Russia, but we find questions constantly arising among Church leaders that require deliberation and discussion, and, often, sanction. One outstanding question was the problem of establishing a theological school and pastors' courses, which are now beginning their work. This question was brought to us by Church leaders. We discussed it, and then submitted our decision to the Council of People's Commissars, which fully approved it. This, by the way, is the only question we have had to carry to the higher authorities.

The decision of the Council of People's Commissars has apparently become a fixed policy, for Mr. Karpov remarked that "if the question were raised of opening more schools, we would see no reason to oppose it."

The extent to which the government is at present inclined to conciliate the Church is shown in Karpov's statement:

Like all Soviet citizens, priests are subject to mobilization. But whenever a case was brought to us where mobilization deprived believers of religious leadership, we have succeeded in getting the priest released from service, and we intend to act so in the future.

Karpov also describes the procedure by which churches may be reopened:

If a group of believers—it does not matter how many—want a church, they sign a petition and refer it to the local church or government leaders. The local soviet takes it up with our representative, who examines the case and refers it, in turn, to us. Any number of people can sign a petition, but a minimum of twenty is needed to establish the legality of a congregation under law. Only occasionally do we turn down petitions for new churches. This is in cases where there is no church building available, and no immediate prospects of constructing one. Sometimes, too, the people in a small hamlet where there are already two or three churches want another. We feel that they cannot possibly get enough money to operate and for that reason their application is rejected.

Patriarch Alexei announced in *Izvestia* before his election that over 200 churches had been reopened in the previous year, and Metropolitan Benjamin on his return from Moscow "estimated that there are about 70 dioceses in Russia at present, served by 45 or 50 bishops." Karpov made the remarkable statement that there are now more churches and more priests in Russia than before the war.

In September, 1945 two remarkable decrees gave substance to the state's new attitude to the Church. By the first, approximately one half of the property confiscated in 1923 has been restored. By the second, ancient shrines were restored.

A notable relaxation in the application of the law on freedom of conscience to education is observable in Mr. Karpov's remarks. He points out that though religion may not be taught in the public schools, parents are free to instruct their own children at home and that "children of any number of parents may also gather or be gathered together in groups to receive religious instruction." In Karpov's view such groups might meet in churches provided the instruction was "purely informative." Restrictions in the printing and sale of religious literature, which was one of the purposes of the amendment to the decree on freedom of conscience, have been removed. Karpov flatly declared that the Orthodox Church may "print whatever it wishes" and stated that his council had given "explicit permission for the Church to order any quantity of Testaments, prayer books and liturgical books, and are ready to facilitate this step in every way even to the extent of making representations to the paper rationing authorities."

2. Two elements stand out in the *sobor* of January, 1945: its broad scope and careful planning, and its results. It is evident that the Soviet Council on Orthodox Affairs and the Church authorities were equally convinced of the desirability of making the *sobor* a turning point in the history of Orthodoxy under Soviet rule. Current problems were attacked with a long range view. The period of emergency was over, that of reconstruction had begun. Co-operation was advantageous to both sides. The position of the state was clear; it had decided to meet the revival of religion halfway. The time was not ripe for atheism and the war had excited religious feeling. It was a bold but prudent course to bring the situation into the open and to supervise the advance of the Church by collaborating with it.

An important feature of the new council was its canonical regularity. The sessions of the *sobor* of 1917 which had elected Tikhon to the patriarchate had coincided with the outbreak of revolution and in consequence had not mustered a quorum. The council which had elected Sergius was also anomalous through the absence of lay electors. Enemies of the patriarchate, especially among the emigrant groups, had capitalized on these inconvenient facts and marshaled them as justification of their aloofness from the Church operating under Soviet rule. Even the *de facto* recognition of Sergius by other patriarchs of the East had of necessity dispensed with the traditional formalities. Telegrams and letters lacked the impressiveness of personal visits and participation in the ceremonies of consecration. Great care, therefore, was taken to make the new *sobor* conform in all respects to the canons. Forty-four Russian dioceses were represented by three delegates each, a bishop, a priest, and a layman. At Alexei's consecration the patriarchs of Antioch, Alexandria, Jerusalem, and Georgia were present and Alexei was permitted by the government to pay them return visits as soon as the matter could be arranged.

The most important result of the *sobor* was the election of a new patriarch to succeed Sergius. Upon the death of the old patriarch, Alexei, Metropolitan of Leningrad and Novgorod, was appointed patriarch locum tenens. At the council he was elected patriarch with the approval of the government mediated through the Soviet Council on Orthodox Affairs. Alexei's secular name was Sergius Vladimirovich Simansky. In his youth he had studied law and received his degree from the University of Moscow in 1899. He then turned to theology and graduated with a doctorate from the Moscow Theological Seminary in 1904. Like Sergius he was a scholar as well as a churchman, had made a name for himself as a Church historian, and had been active in formulating the new curriculum for the reopened theological school at Moscow. In 1921 he became vicar of Leningrad and bishop of Yamburg and in 1923, metropolitan of Novgorod. In 1933 he returned to Leningrad with the title of Metropolitan of Leningrad and Novgorod.

The choice of Alexei from an ecclesiastical point of view was a natural one both in view of the prestige of his see and of his proved ability and close relations with his predecessor. He was a man of conservative antecedents in family and education and these considerations were not likely to commend him to Soviet politicians. The latter, however, knew him as a popular figure whose heroic leadership had been an important asset in the siege of Leningrad and who had proved his adherence to Sergius' policy toward the state by effective utterances and by raising large sums of money for defense funds under the most difficult circumstances. He was therefore a man to be trusted alike by Church and State, uncompromisingly loyal to Orthodoxy and to Russia, and one who had shared to the full the trials of the revolutionary period and the most acute sufferings of the war.

It was clear to Alexei and his advisers that the position of the Moscow patriarchate, once regularized, could best be strengthened by the unification of Russian Orthodoxy at home and abroad. Little information is available on the fate of the dissident factions like the Living Church in Russia since the outbreak of the war. They appear to have lost their vitality and influence and it may be presumed that their future is precarious.

Opposition to the Moscow patriarchate was most vocal in emigrant colonies abroad, especially in Paris, Yugoslavia, and the United States. It lies outside the scope of this book to trace the history of Russian Orthodoxy in the Emigration. The pattern of ecclesiastical attachments and divergences, the underlying personal attractions and repulsions, have been extremely complex. Old feuds, temporary and local circumstances, and wide differences in social and political feeling have played a large part in creating and perpetuating chaos. A reason, if not an excuse, for this situation has been the actual uncertainty of the destiny of the patriarchal Church in Russia and the extent it would be compelled to compromise with the state to maintain its existence. The news from Russia was always fragmentary, usually prejudiced and difficult to interpret as a whole. It was hard for people whose memories of the Bolshevik persecution of religion were fresh and bitter to put faith in a Church whose relations with the Soviet regime appeared increasingly amiable. An analogy with the Deutsche Christen and the futile figure of Reichbischof Müller suggested itself. The strategy of the Russian hierarchy with the state was viewed not in its actual context but from the point of view of its implications for *émigrés,* many of whom had become citizens of other countries.

This tension was particularly great in the United States where the government had openly declared its hostility to Communism and strictly enforced regulations against its propaganda. The Serbian group was under leadership which at the Synod of Karlowitz had in effect declared a holy war on the Soviets and declared the Church in Russia devoid of competent leadership. The position of Metropolitan Eulogius in Paris was hardly less strained.

In spite of these difficulties the *sobor* of 1945 went quietly and effectively about the business of allaying suspicion and reuniting dissident elements. The emigrant church in Paris has recognized the patriarch of Moscow first through the mediation of the patriarch of Constantinople, then directly, and relations with the Mother Church have been restored. The Russians in Yugoslavia have also been reconciled.

3. The problem of Russian Orthodoxy in America is complicated by a number of factors, some natural outgrowths of Orthodox life in the United States, some intrusive. The great majority of Russian Orthodox parishes in America accept the jurisdiction of the Archbishop Theophilus who, with his advisers, has so far refused to unite with the patriarchal see of Moscow. A small group of parishes accept the Metropolitan Benjamin who is the accredited representative of the Moscow patriarchate in this country and holds the title of Metropolitan of the Aleutian Islands and North America. The situation in 1942 is thus described in *The Truth about Religion in Russia*:

The metropolitan of North America, Platon, (Rozhdestvenskii) assumed in 1929 the canonical jurisdiction of Metropolitan Sergius as head of the Russian Orthodox Church but in 1933 repudiated the Mother Church and on his own authority established an autonomous North American eparchy. For this act he was delated to the court of archbishops, August 16, 1933 and deprived of ecclesiastical functions.

After his death in 1934 his successors elected in his place Bishop

Theophilus who with his council supported the independent autonomy of the American Church. Thereupon all bishops of this ecclesiastically dissident persuasion, with Theophilus at their head, were declared January 4, 1935, subject to the same judgment and deposition as the Metropolitan Platon. In 1935 the followers of Platon united with adherents of the Synod of Karlowitz who had also been deposed. Meanwhile, from 1933 to the present there has resided in North America the patriarchal exarch in America appointed by the Moscow Patriarchate, Metropolitan Benjamin (Phedchenkov), directing the Aleutian and North American eparchy and all Orthodox churches in the U. S. A. loyal to their mother, the Russian Church.

It can be seen that a situation of considerable delicacy had been created by these canonical aberrations and the matter seems not to have been eased by attempts at *rapprochement* between the two groups. It was, however, decided to invite representatives of the Theophilist group to the *sobor* in Moscow, and after some deliberation the invitation was accepted. It had been greatly hoped that Theophilus himself might attend, but pleading ill health he remained in America and sent two representatives, Bishop Alexei of Sitka, Alaska, and The Very Reverend J. O. Dzvonchik, secretary of the Metropolitan (i.e., Theophilist) Council of the Russian Church in America. Negotiations were opened but broke down and the Theophilist representatives returned to America with the breach unhealed. Since that time Archbishop Alexei of Rostov and Yaroslav has appeared in this country as patriarchal representative. It may be presumed that his principal mission is to continue the conversations begun in Moscow.

It is impossible for an outsider to gauge the undercurrents in a situation so intricate and so charged with theological and personal animus. It is difficult to see how Russian Orthodoxy in America can establish an autonomy which will hold and be accepted by the rest of the Orthodox world on the basis of such irregular canonical procedures as gave rise to the Theophilist Church in this country. The last twenty-five years have been a period of great irregularity in Church discipline within Orthodoxy, but the recent trend in and outside Russia has been to correct anomalies and restore old and established ties. In America the Theophilists are in an impressive majority. However, they represent a small fraction of the Orthodox world and are not likely to achieve permanent success by pursuing a course found impractical in France and Yugoslavia and condemned not only by the see of Moscow, but by the other patriarchs of the Eastern Church. A schism may be large, but it remains a schism.

The Theophilists on their part obviously fear the specter of the Moscow state behind the Moscow Church. In its eagerness to express appreciation of the toleration it now enjoys, the patriarchal Church does not seem to have envisaged clearly the position of members of the Russian Orthodox Church who have either migrated or been born abroad, and whose religion is a thing quite independent of their attitude toward Soviet Russia's political and social system. On the theory (a) that the powers that be are ordained of God, (b) that the patriarchal Church has recognized the Soviet state as the *de facto* government of Russia, and (c) that the Soviet state is intolerant of criticism and opposition within its borders, it is natural that the patriarchal Church should encourage its members in Russia to be loyal to the government of the U.S.S.R., and to abstain from subversive action and hostile criticism. It is difficult to see how these recommendations can obtain outside Russia and how Americans can accept orders from Russians of whatever ecclesiastical rank in matters affecting political sympathies and action. It must in some way be made clear that if Russian Orthodoxy is to remain a unity, that unity is to be one of faith and not of politics. There is a movement in American Orthodoxy to scrap ethnic traditions and to enter upon a new phase of

American cultural unity. The use of English, instead of Russian, Greek, and Arabic in the Liturgy, the reconciliation of old differences between the various branches of Orthodoxy in Europe and the Near East, would do much to accomplish this. Generations of Americans are growing up with Russian, Greek, Syrian, Bulgarian, Rumanian, and Serbian blood in their veins but whose one hope of a common religious bond lies in re-interpreting its significance in terms of their adopted culture. It may be that differences between Theophilists and Benjamites will be submerged in this larger movement of faith and order.

4. The relations between the Russian Church and other communions, except the Roman Catholics, have improved since the war. Through the efforts of the Ecumenical Movement and of various Anglican organizations designed to promote friendly relations with Orthodoxy easy access has been established from both sides. Patriarch Alexei, upon his election, received greetings from the Archbishop of Canterbury and the Presiding Bishop of the Protestant Episcopal Church in America, and from the Federal Council of Churches. The Archbishop of York, Dr. Garbett and the dean of Canterbury, England's outstanding champion of Russia, have paid friendly visits to Russia. Similar visits from American churchmen are planned when conditions become propitious. The importance of these gestures for stimulating good will and steadying public sentiment between Russia and her allies is obvious. Their ecclesiastical implications can easily be exaggerated.

The relations between the Russian Church and the Vatican have not improved. Advices from the Religious News Service have given evidence of attempts to resolve differences, but as yet nothing encouraging has taken place. This is not surprising for three reasons. *First,* theological differences and the theological temper of Roman Catholicism and Russian Orthodoxy remain unaffected by the Russian Revolution and the two great wars. One of Patriarch Sergius' last utterances contained a denunciation of papal claims, but the issues of controversy were in no sense novel. It is unlikely that a schism which was begun in the ninth century and which has withstood the upheavals of a thousand troubled years of European history will be repaired by the revival of the patriarchal Church in Russia at the present time.

Second, the revival of Christianity in Russia during and since the war has been closely interwoven with the revival of Russian national feeling. The Vatican's attacks on Communism as a social philosophy since the days of Leo XIII cannot be ignored and cannot serve at the present time as anything but an irritation in the relations between the patriarchal Church and Rome. Roman Catholic pressure was exerted in behalf of Franco and against the Communists in whose ranks many Russians fought and died in the Spanish civil war. There was no break between the Church and the Italian state during this last war, and the concordat between the Vatican and German Fascism, honored mostly in the breach, was largely the work of the papal secretary of state, Pacelli, now Pope Pius XII. In a cooler atmosphere and at a greater distance these facts may fall into place with others, a calmer view may be taken, and sounder judgments passed, but the time is not opportune and sentiment is not prepared for mutual confidence between Russian Orthodoxy and the Roman Church.

Third, the Vatican, the Soviet government, and the Russian Church are keeping a watchful eye on territories recently dominated by the U.S.S.R. in which a large proportion of the population is Roman Catholic. From the Roman point of view it is imperative that the religious interests of these people be safeguarded and that the faithful should not be encouraged to shift their allegiance to some other form of Christianity or to lapse into atheism. From the Soviet point of view it is imperative that political issues in these areas, notably in Poland, should not be obscured by religious ones nor expedient action hampered by ecclesiastical influences not amenable to state control. From the Orthodox point of view Roman propaganda should be countered whenever and wherever possible by Orthodox action, especially where Slavic peoples are concerned.

In an article for the Religious News Service, March 14, 1945, Professor Timasheff wrote:

Urgent reasons for a Soviet-Vatican understanding can be seen in the religious composition of present Soviet territory. Prior to 1939, there were almost no Catholics in the Soviet Union, and the Vatican's attitude toward the Russian government was dictated by the antireligious policy and propaganda of the latter. The annexations of the years 1939–40 brought under Soviet dominance large areas with Catholic populations. At a conservative estimate, eight million Catholics are now under Soviet rule. Moreover, the Soviet armies occupy the whole of Poland, with her preponderantly Catholic population, and two-thirds of Hungary where Catholics form the majority. They dominate the Balkans, and, in some parts of the peninsula, they are within another battlefield between East and West, Orthodox and Catholic. Bulgaria is entirely Orthodox, but in Rumania, Catholics are numerous. Thus, despite attacks on the Vatican by the Moscow press and radio, and by the Russian Orthodox Church, there is a practical problem involved which demands some form of agreement between the Russian state and the Holy See.

This, again, is a long range view. At present the areas where the Orthodox-Roman sensibilities are the most ruffled, political competition is at its keenest. Major political decisions must be made and secured before the religious question can be treated reasonably or fairly. In this matter the Soviet government can be expected to act with the utmost firmness and caution. Premature concessions to Roman claims and wishes, however justified by historical precedent or immediate religious need, are unlikely to be made.

INDEX